What Others Are Saying

Diane Gardner bravely shows us how to keep presumption from sabotaging our faith and thwarting our destiny. Read this book and learn how to recognize and overcome your presumptions.

Deborah Smith Pegues, Bestselling Author, Speaker, CPA *Forgive, Let Go, and Live;* and *30 Days to Taming Your Tongue* www.confrontingissues.com

Unmet expectations can be the root of much of our unhappiness and grief. We often blame God when the fault actually lies with us. In our finite wisdom, we presume things to be totally different from what they actually are. This is an issue we all struggle with, and it is dealt with remarkably well in Diane Gardner's book, *Increase Your Capacity to Hear From God: Stop Walking in Presumption.* If you have found yourself presuming things to be true that proved not to be, this is a must-read.

Susan Titus Osborn, Bestselling author of over 30 books including *Breaking Invisible Chains* www.christiancommunicator.com

Diane Gardner unearths the secret thoughts we hold deep in our hearts. Then we often make God accountable for them when He never said those things in the first place! We cause our own disappointments because we let our secret imaginations carry us to a level God never intended.

This book is not Christianity 101, but is a message for those hungering and thirsting after truth, who are willing to search their hearts to be truly set free. I love the story of Naaman and especially how Rev. Gardner dissects the story. Like us, Naaman presumed to know exactly what, when, where, and through whom God would act. He got his feelings hurt when God didn't do what he expected. When our secret expectations are not met, we are disappointed and can get angry with God. But if we humble ourselves like Naaman, and are brutally honest with ourselves and with God, we will find true freedom. Diane shows us how to overcome the consequences of these negative emotions.

Joyce Sloss, Co-Founder and Managing Partner SCA Strategic Partnership International, LLC
www.scastrategic.com

INCREASE YOUR CAPACITY TO HEAR FROM GOD

Stop Walking in Presumption

Diane Gardner

Published by God's House of Favor Publishing Co.

ISBN 978-0-9967636-0-8

Introduction

I feel sometimes as though God wants to increase the level of truth I currently can handle. I desire truth as *He says it*, not only as *I see it*.

Often I say, "Lord, Help me know Your truth!"

I decided the best way for me to cooperate with the Lord was to get a specific plan from Him.

So I prayed, "God, I'd like You to give me a strategy that saves me from *myself*. Give me a truth which shows me when I'm headed in the wrong direction and I think it's right. I want to be rescued from walking in presumption and never let it have dominion over me."

The strategy He revealed has rescued me. This truth has lit my path when I found myself walking in presumption and I thought surely I was headed the right way. I've shared this truth with countless others and as they examined their hearts and they speak this as an affirmation of truth their perception shifted.

You can do the same and increase your capacity to receive truth and hear from God.

Today I choose to:

Love God.
Love God's Truth.
Love God's Word.
More than I love being right in my own eyes,
And more than I love having my own way.

Table of Contents

Acknowledgments

I am grateful to God for surrounding my life with quality people. People of prayer are those who mean the most to me.

Thank you, family, for your prayers: Carlton, Kisha, Johnny, Dana, and others.

Special thanks to my prayer sisters of Christian Women in Media and Women United in Ministry who are peers that cover me and help me stay encouraged.

My ACOB core support team is the best. You know who you are, and every time I am rewarded for changing a life through this book, you will be too. Also thanks to my growing list of ministry prayer and financial partners near and far.

Great appreciation goes to my financial sponsors Joyce and Georgia.

Thanks to my coach and fearless leader of our "Best Seller" team, Kathleen Mailer. My backside is still burning from all the fires you lit under me.

Most of all, this book was made possible through the person who takes my raw mess and helps me make it into a message, Susan Titus Osborn.

And thank you to the person who first believed in my ability to write, my friend and ministry partner, Liberty Savard.

Also thank you to the one who has assigned *herself* the "job" of keeping me on task, Deborah Smith Pegues, who I first shared that the message on presumption was burning in my heart, and she agreed it should become a book.

Now the book is here, and I am grateful for you who will read it and receive from it the passion and love I have for you.

What Is Presumption Anyway?

Chapter One

Keep back Your servant also from presumptuous sins; Let them not have dominion over me.

Then I shall be blameless, And I shall be innocent of great transgression (Psalm 19:13).

Have you ever thought you knew how an important prayer was going to be answered? Did you think you had it all figured out, but later realized the truth was nothing like you had reasoned things to be? If your answer was yes, then you were being presumptuous because of unmet expectations.

To presume means to believe something to be true: to accept that something is almost certain to be correct even though there is no proof of it, or that it is extremely likely. It means to seem to prove something. It also means to behave arrogantly, overconfidently, or disrespectfully by doing something you are not entitled to do. You have overstepped your bounds.

When you realized God's plan was not your plan, how did you react? Was it with anger, tears, resignation, or even laughter? How did you handle your disappointment with God? Did you give Him the silent treatment? Did you cry for a while? Or did you become angry and take out your frustration on others? Oh, you have never been disappointed with God? Then you may not be looking closely at what is going on inside you. Sometimes it's hard to admit our disappointment with God.

Even Jesus wanted things to be different from what His Father had planned. Look at His prayer in the Garden of Gethsemane.

O My Father, if it is possible, let this cup pass from Me; nevertheless, not as I will, but as You will (Matthew 26:39b).

Jesus prayed to let this cup pass from Him because He was hoping His Father had come up with another plan for salvation. I believe the human side of Jesus wanted our redemption to come about in a less painful way.

Naaman was commander of the Syrian army, but He could no longer go to battle for the king because he had contracted leprosy, a highly contagious disease.

Then Naaman went with his horses and chariot, and he stood at the door of Elisha's house. And Elisha sent Gehazi his messenger to him, saying, *"Go and wash in the Jordan seven times, and your flesh shall be restored to you, and you shall be clean."* But Naaman became furious, and went away and said, *"Indeed, I said to myself, 'He will surely come out to me, and stand and call on the name of the Lord his God, and wave his hand over the place, and heal the leprosy...So he turned and went away in a rage* (2 Kings 5:9-12).

Naaman turned away in *anger* when God's way of healing him did not live up to his expectations. To be healed he was to dip seven times in a nasty river. Elisha disappointed him further by not even showing up to administer the healing to him; instead Elisha sent his servant Gehazi.

A servant of Naaman's suggested he humble himself and obey the prophet's instructions. Naaman recovered from his presumption, obeyed, and was healed.

Jesus said, "But after I have been raised, I will go before you to Galilee."

Peter said to Him, "Even if all are made to stumble, yet I will not be."

Jesus said to him, "Assuredly, I say to you that today, even this night, before the rooster crows twice, you will deny Me three times."

But he spoke more vehemently, "If I have to die with You, I will not deny You!"

And they all said likewise (John 18:28-31).

But again he denied with an oath, "I do not know the Man!"

And the servant girl saw him again, and began to say to those who stood by, "This is one of them." But he denied it again.

And a little later those who stood by said to Peter again, "Surely you are one of them; for you are a Galilean, and your speech shows it."

Then he began to curse and swear, "I do not know this Man of whom you speak!"

A second time the rooster crowed. Then Peter called to mind the word that Jesus had said to him, "Before the rooster crows twice, you will deny Me three times." And when he thought about it, he wept (Mark 14:69-72).

Peter presumed he would stand with Jesus to the end, but he failed Jesus miserably, denying Him. The Scripture says Peter *wept bitterly.*

Peter recovered from His presumption, which had led to his denial. Jesus forgave and restored Peter and he became the leading apostle.

Jesus rose from the dead and showed Himself to two women and then the disciples. The apostle Thomas was not there when the resurrected Messiah appeared in the room.

Apostle Thomas was deeply devoted to Jesus. When Jesus died Thomas had his hopes dashed. He thought surely Jesus was the Messiah. Afterwards it was hard for him to recover and believe Jesus had risen from the dead, even though Jesus had plainly said He would rise from the dead after three days. Do you think Thomas must have presumed those words meant something else? Thomas' response sounds to me like he had *resigned* himself to living with the feeling of hopelessness.

Now Thomas, called the Twin, one of the twelve, was not with them when Jesus came. The other disciples therefore said to him, "We have seen the Lord."

So he said to them, "Unless I see in His hands the print of the nails, and put my finger into the print of the nails, and put my hand into His side, I will not believe."

And after eight days His disciples were again inside, and Thomas with them. Jesus came, the doors being shut, and stood in the midst, and said, "Peace to you!" Then He said to Thomas, "Reach your finger here, and look at My hands; and reach your hand here, and put it into My side. Do not be unbelieving, but believing."

And Thomas answered and said to Him, "My Lord and my God!" (John 20:24-28).

Apostle Thomas recovered from His presumption when he came face to face with the truth about his sense of hopelessness and lack of faith.

On a recent group prayer call I participate in weekly I heard the frustration in the voice of someone on the other end. I didn't know the story behind this heart-felt petition from one of the Christian Women in Media on the line, but something must have gone very wrong. "Lord, I've *got* to know when I'm presuming. Help me to understand how to deal with my unmet expectations. I need to know what to do."

The woman who shared the request had recognized that presuming was the insidious foundation to her recent disappointment. Compassion filled my heart as I felt her anguish as she prayed. Our focus turned to other prayer requests, and we continued praying, but I was thinking about her request when our call ended.

My eyes filled with tears as I hung up the phone and thought about how, when we presume, sometimes it can bring such pain to our hearts.

I prayed for her, "God help presumption not have dominion over her. Cleanse her from this secret fault and bring her to truth and faith. Thank you for giving her the wisdom to see the source of her disappointment. Help her to release this disappointment. Renew her mind and heal her heart. Lord, help me to get the truth You've taught me about presumption into the hands and hearts of many like her. Amen."

Presumption is an ingredient we can add to God's truth. It spoils the faith God uses to answer our prayers. Unmet expectations can be recognized by a key phrase: *I thought*, or *I thought surely*. We need to be careful not to assume we know what God's answer is.

Joy Dawson spoke to a few thousand women at Angelus Temple in Los Angeles for Women on the Front Line on the dangers of presumption. She quoted from her book, *Forever Ruined for the Ordinary.* (This book was required reading for those in my ministry). She strongly warned us, "Guard against presumption until God gives us His full understanding. When we are convinced that God is utterly righteous, true, and faithful in our circumstances, we should simply say, 'Lord, I do not understand the outcome of what *I thought* were steps of obedience I've taken to obey You. But because Your character is flawless and You are faithful, I believe You will give me understanding about Your ways in time.' That is the true response of humility and faith."

She encouraged us to pay more attention to the simple thoughts we have that can be from God and could be a step into our destiny. Oh how often I have successfully followed that slight impression and yet, how often I overrode it considering the thought insignificant.

Some also consider me an authority on presumption and how it can be played out in our lives. I certainly have presumed enough to fill several books with only my presumptive errors. I have been studying the Scriptures on the subject, along with human behavior and the consequences when we presume. I've spoken on the subject nationally and internationally.

The first teaching I heard on this subject was by Dr. Jerry Savelle, a Texas evangelist at the time, who came to Riverside, California, and spoke at a church back around 1976. He said, "Presumption is a roadblock to your faith. It's something that is always with us so we have to learn when to take it serious. In the Old Testament God showed the seriousness of speaking presumptuously; it could get you stoned."

Now the man who acts presumptuously and will not heed the priest who stands to minister there before the Lord your God, or the judge, that man shall die. So you shall put away the evil from Israel. And all the people shall hear and fear, and no longer act presumptuously (Deuteronomy 17:12-14).

Shortly after that a pastor friend from Crenshaw Christian Center in Los Angeles, Dr Fred K. C. Price wrote a book exposing *Faith, Foolishness or Presumption.*

Faith is a way of life, not something you use only when you get in trouble. If that is the way we are to live, then when we are not living in faith, we are living in presumption or foolishness.

Romans 1:17 tells us faith is the core substance we live by: *For in it the righteousness of God is revealed from faith to faith; as it is written, "The just shall live by faith."*

I sat mesmerized with Evangelist Savelle's sermon and astonished with Dr. Price's book and sermon. As the principles of presumption were laid open to my understanding, I realized presumption was the way I handled my entire life. I presumed on God, myself, and everyone else. As a result I stayed disappointed and offended with God, myself, and everyone else, especially my husband, and children. When it came to God I had many prayers answered, but the ones that were not answered I had no clue as to why not. So I sought Him for understanding.

I have learned to respect how important it is for me to recognize my own presumptions and take charge to overcome the consequences. I know one of the reasons I'm alive today and in basically good health is because I work to overcome presumption when it rears its ugly head. I fight the fight of faith to have dominion over presumptions. It remains a part of my life, but I choose to overcome it. When I sense an impression to do something concerning my body, I do what I can to follow that inward impression or gut feeling. I try not to override the impression with my presumption.

Yet, after becoming an authority on the subject, I still constantly presume, especially when it comes to receiving answers to my prayers. When will I ever stop the cycle of presumption? I'll probably have to wait until I enter heaven. There is no guessing in heaven; we will have instant answers.

Dear friends, now we are children of God, and what we will be has not yet been made known. But we know that when Christ appears, we shall be like him, for we shall see him as he is (1 John 3:2).

There is no way to go through life without presuming at times. Why? We are thinkers, and we reason ourselves into a decision. We draw conclusions with little or no facts to back us up. Such is the state of every human being. I'm strapped with being a rational, intelligent, curious human being who always wants to know what the final outcome of everything is going to be. What we can do is learn how to *stop walking in presumption* as our life's foundation.

Do you have a busy mind? My mind doesn't rest until I can settle something or give my mind an assignment. Until there is a satisfactory conclusion to how a prayer or situation is going to be resolved I keep thinking of conclusions. Even in everyday life, if I see something that I don't understand what happened, I make up something that makes sense to me. I constantly judge myself and others when the Bible says don't judge. I had no clue how to stop judging until I studied presumption. Now when I presume on someone and make a judgment, I stop in my tracks and tell myself to stop it. Then I think, *Diane, you are presuming, and you don't know that as a fact. Instead of judging, I take that moment to pray for that person.*

This same human trait is the basis for our worry. Presumption and worry are intertwined, but in the midst of our presumption and worry, we can choose not to allow them to rule our lives. I share later in the book the steps on how to become an overcomer.

Bill Johnson

At the Leadershift Conference at HRock Church in Pasadena, California, Bill Johnson taught, "One of the main cornerstones of thought is that we choose to have a tangible awareness of His goodness and we live like it.

"Many that say, 'Yes, God is good,' also credit Him with every disaster and crisis all over the world. We have confused God's *ability* to *redeem* a situation with His *ability* to *author* a situation. And they are not the same. Being able to make that distinction in our thinking, I think, is the cornerstone of all theology—the goodness of God.

"This is Kingdom Culture we can daily walk in and see God move. We can live from the presence of the King and His goodness and lead an intentional life," concluded Bill.

Not long ago I was ministering in another country when a woman who had purchased a signed copy of my book *Overcoming the Enemy's Storms* asked for prayer. As she shared I saw she was presuming. She told me, and those in the room, she and her husband had been divorced for eight years. She had believed in reconciliation this whole time, but recently he had gotten remarried.

"Everyone knows I wanted reconciliation, but now he's married," she said with a tone of frustration in her voice.

Throwing up her hands she asked, "Should I keep waiting to see if the marriage lasts? What about all the encouraging words the Lord spoke to me about us and ministry together? Why didn't anything God said come to pass?" she asked.

I answered her hard questions by saying, "Let's pray and ask God. I don't have the answers but God does."

We prayed until I heard from God. "I believe the Lord has answered you. God said during those eight years you were so focused on your former husband that you built your whole relationship with God around those prayers and your presumed answer."

I rose from my chair to put my hand on her shoulder. "God said in order to preserve your relationship with Him whenever God wanted to encourage you He referred to something concerning you and your husband getting back together. You wanted your husband to return home so badly that you *limited* your relationship with God to only that subject. You were obsessed and presumed your union was God's main focus also.

"God loves you so much, so He did what you required. Now your former husband has remarried, and you know that door is closed. The Lord wants to rebuild His relationship with you as His precious daughter so you and He can be reconciled and have a new beginning."

She scooted to the end of her chair and exclaimed, "You are right! I didn't want to hear anything else. I'm ready to have a new relationship with my heavenly Father!"

We prayed and broke the consequences of her long term presumption by speaking against the words of bondage she and others spoke over her and him. We also renounced any deception she had experienced. She surrendered her mind. She embraced the love of the Father God anew. She left there with a big smile, a new joy, and my book in her hand to guide her to overcome her presumptions and move forward.

God is so good to communicate with us on the level we require even when we have been presuming for years.

Recently I received an understanding that overwhelmed me and filled me with even more gratitude. In my spirit I heard these words:

Tell my children that I am God, and I have all of the ability that name represents. I'm omnipotent, all powerful, and almighty. I have the power to answer their prayers.

But I do not answer one prayer because I'm God. That is my ability.

Every prayer I answer is because I'm their Father. I want to answer their prayers because I love each one as their Father. I have the love and individual care of a loving, perfect Father.

Jesus did not say He came to reveal God. He said He came to reveal to us the Father. In the Old Testament they experienced God although some learned to embrace Him as Jehovah—the covenant-making, covenant keeping-God. He was not Father because Christ had not come. Today He is our Creator only until we embrace Christ as our Savior, and we become sons of God and we are adopted by the Father.

Jesus prayed to the Father for us as He closed His earthly ministry in John 17:25-26: *O righteous Father! The world has not known You, but I have known You; and these have known that You sent Me. And I have declared to them Your name, and will declare it, that the love with which You loved Me may be in them, and I in them.*

Naaman Added Presumption to His Faith

Chapter Two

But Naaman became furious, and went away and said, "Indeed, I said to myself, 'He will surely come out to me, and stand and call on the name of the Lord his God, and wave his hand over the place, and heal the leprosy" (2 Kings 5:11).

I'm convinced next to salvation the second greatest miracle in our spiritual life is a changed perception. This changed perception often altars our prayer life for the good, and subsequently in that particular area it forms a new trajectory of our walk with Christ. Such a dramatic change happened to me in

1976 when I heard a sermon on Naaman's presumption. Two years later I heard another sermon and read two books on the theme of faith and presumption.

I changed from a life of perpetual presumptions, to a life of faith as I grew in my capacity to hear from God. Prior to my embrace of this truth, my life was filled with constant anxiety. Afterwards I changed to a person of perpetual mercy and forgiveness for myself and others when we presumed. Although I still presumed regularly, I recognized it and did my best not to allow it to take dominion over my thoughts and my behavior.

I acted on an antidote that helped me come up with a plan of eight steps to full recovery, which I will share with you later. First, here is the biblical story of Naaman that to this day challenges my life. I hope you never forget his story either.

Naaman was the top military leader of the Syrian army, but could not serve because he had become a leper. He heard God healed people through a prophet in Israel, Elisha. In faith he went to find the prophet to get healed. It didn't go down the way Naaman had hoped. Being a man of such important stature, distinction, and pride, Naaman felt disrespected by the prophet, Elisha who would not come out to pray for him. Naaman left angry. His servant reasoned with him, and Naaman eventually humbled himself and washed in the nasty Jordan River (which is still an important, but nasty looking river today. I chose not to be baptized in the Jordan when I was in Israel. I understood Naaman's resistance). But he dipped seven times and was healed.

His presuming almost cost him his miracle, and would have cost him his life. I want to take this story section, by section so we can see the spiritual principles that will revolutionize how we perceive God, faith, and presumption.

What is leprosy? How does it affect you? Leprosy is a tropical skin and nerve disease. Its incubation period can be 1-30 years. It is transmitted by close personal contact with someone who has it. When a leper dies everything is burned: clothes, eating utensils, and everything they have touched. In severe cases there is a loss of sensation in extremities, and disfigurement like the nose, ears, fingers, and toes which flesh may be eaten away—sometimes even the bones. A leper is immediately isolated from all non-leprous contact. They can never touch their spouse, children, or another human again except another leper. There is no cure.

With this understanding I can imagine Naaman's wife crying about the "loss" of her husband. The maid heard her mistress's words and felt her heartache concerning this.

I'm amazed at the faith and heart of this maiden. Naaman had captured her and taken her away from everything familiar. Now she worked as a slave, which meant she would never have anything of her own and was separated from her family. She could have been bitter at Naaman because directly or indirectly he was the cause of her captivity. She could easily have wanted Naaman, her captor, to die. Instead she had mercy on him.

Now Naaman, commander of the army of the king of Syria, was a great and honorable man in the eyes of his master, because by him the LORD had given victory to Syria. He was also a mighty man of valor, but he was a leper. And the Syrians had gone out on raids, and had brought back captive a young girl from the land of Israel. She waited on Naaman's wife. Then she said to her mistress, "If only my master [the king] *were with the prophet who is in Samaria! For he would heal him of his leprosy." And Naaman went in and told his master, saying, "Thus and thus said the girl who is from the land of Israel."*

Then the king of Syria said, "Go now, and I will send a letter to the king of Israel" (2 Kings 5:1-5).

We see faith in action from everyone in this story. The maiden, Naaman's wife, Naaman, and the King of Syria:

- The maiden believed in the healing power of God: action—told her boss's wife

- Naaman's wife believed: action—told Naaman to pursue his healing
- Naaman believed his wife: action—took a risk and spoke to the king of Syria
- The king believed: action—sent a letter, money, and a delegation with Naaman

What is faith? The belief in, or trust in somebody or something. Faith is that belief in action. Faith must be acted upon.

Hebrews 11:1 in the Amplified says, *Now faith is the assurance (confirmation, the title deed) of the things [we] hope for, being the proof of things [we] do not see and the conviction of their reality [faith perceiving as real fact what is not been revealed to the senses].*

Faith is the foundation substance we need to stand firm. It also requires action to be real biblical faith. James 2:17 says, *Thus also faith by itself, if it does not have works, is dead.*

Faith comes by hearing and the follow through of corresponding actions. The powerful Romans 10:17 shows us how we obtain faith and how to get more: *So then faith comes by hearing and hearing by the Word of God.*

The word *hearing* in this particular verse is not simply listening to words; it is the same root word as *obedience*, and obedience demands action. So it is hearing in such a way that you must act. Like Jesus said many times, including Mark 4:9, *And he said unto them, He that hath ears to hear, let him hear.* The meaning is deeper than simply hearing words. He was speaking to those willing to take action on the words they heard.

Hebrews 4:2b says, *but the word which they* (Israelites in the wilderness) *heard did not profit them, not being mixed with faith in those who heard it.* In other words they did not act on the words they heard. This provoked God to disappointment and anger.

I have no clue how long it took Naaman to arrive at Elisha's door. Did it take a day, two days, or a week? However long it took his faith grew. He was totally convinced he was going to be healed when He got there, no doubt about it. But something happened in the dark corners of Naaman's meditations. He thought again and again about the 5 Ws and 1 H of presumption: who, what, when, where, why, and how God will answer his request. He came up with plan after plan until he found the one he liked the best. He chose a plan, which fitted his pride, his personality, and saved his dignity in front of the troops.

Naaman filled in the 5 Ws and 1 H of presumption. He said to himself: "Yes, that's the plan I want! Where: At the prophet's door. When: As soon as I arrive. Who: Elisha of course will do this personally because he is the leader and I'm a leader. What: He will stand in front of me and wave his hand over the leprosy spots. How: Call on the name of his God. Why: For me to be healed! " There's his secret fault. Something he added to his faith and by the time he got to Elisha the thing had taken over and was in front of his faith—presumption.

A truth to always remember: when God gives instructions He takes into consideration our heart attitude, as well as what character issues He wants to build in us to help us become a better person. Man looks on the outward appearance but God looks at and shapes the heart.

Then Naaman went with his horses and chariot, and he stood at the door of Elisha's house. And Elisha sent a messenger to him, saying, "Go and wash in the Jordan seven times, and your flesh shall be restored to you, and you shall be clean." But Naaman became furious, and went away and said, Indeed, I said to myself, 'He will surely come out to me, and stand and call on the name of the LORD his God, and wave his hand over the place, and heal the leprosy.' Are not the Abanah and Pharpar, the rivers of Damascus, better than all the waters of Israel? Could I not wash in them and be clean?" So he turned and went away in a rage (2 Kings 5:9-12).

Naaman got offended when things didn't come about the way he presumed. He had one of the typical responses to presumption—anger.

Often in the course of one day we get offended because we've figured out in the hidden meditations of our mind the when, where, what, and through whom of presumption, and then it doesn't turn out the way we thought surely it would. How often do we do this to God? This is a major part of anxiety and internal health issues. Our internal organs don't know the difference between truth and presumption. The stress levels are the same. I believe presumption can be the first spark to ignite worry.

Even though he was angry because of his presumption Naaman did ask a valid question. Much like us when we know God wants something done in a way that hurts our pride and requires a full surrender, we may ask, "Lord, can I do it another way or another time?" We neglect to think that God has already taken everything into consideration before we receive our instructions.

If you can answer this question then take a moment to meditate on the depth of why this is true. Then you will be light-years ahead of others. Why couldn't Naaman wash in the rivers of Damascus if that's all it took for him to get cleansed?

Yes, you are absolutely right. Because the Lord didn't say those rivers! He was not cleansed by the water. We know that. He was cleansed and healed by obeying the Word of the Lord! Jesus said, *You are already clean because of the word that I have spoken to you* (John 15:3).

The Lord's word said the Jordan River, so nowhere else would work for his healing. Jordan River worked because God said so, period. Naaman didn't understand the Word of the Lord and God's ways. God does everything by His Word. We can wonder and reason about a lot of things, but grace works by God's Word. Blessing and rewards are tied to the conditions and/or instructions to be obeyed. He wants us to live by His Word. He will never violate nor altar the Word which He has spoken. Because of this we can have more understanding of what He will and won't do.

Even in His sovereignty we can find the principle of how He operates through His Word. This truth alone can bring us to great peace and answer lifelong questions.

And his servants came near and spoke to him and said, "My father, if the prophet had told you to do something great would you not have done it? How much more then when he says to you 'Wash, and be clean'?" (2 Kings 5:13).

His servants recognized his pride and his presumption. Both must be addressed because our faulty focus has to change to let the faith in us arise. And they came up with a reasonable way to confront (challenge) Naaman into letting go of his presumption and surrendering his pride. His servants were still full of faith.

Are you open to the "wounds of a friend"? Proverbs 27:5-6 has a message for us that is at times hard to swallow. It says, *Open rebuke is better than love carefully concealed. Faithful are the wounds of a friend, but the kisses of an enemy are deceitful.*

Naaman received a dramatically changed perception where his prayer life and his walk with God changed radically. He let go of pride and presumption. Right behind these the truth is waiting to be revealed. If you continue in the truth, then you will be set free.

So he went down and dipped seven times in the Jordan, according to the saying of the man of God; and his flesh was restored like the flesh of a little child, and he was clean. And he returned to the man of God, he and all his aides, and came and stood before him; and he said, "Indeed, now I know that there is no God in all the earth, except in Israel; now therefore, please take a gift from your servant" (II Kings 5:14-15).

Presumption will always be a part of our lives because we are rational thinkers and always reason things out. That's normal, and OK. Become authentic about your presumptions like Naaman eventually did by humbling himself and letting go of what he thought. We may need someone to point the truth out to us, as Naaman's servant did, maybe a friend, family, or even a stranger.

Let's pray in light of what we've learned through Naaman.

Father, thank You, I desire this clear example of faith and presumption to change my perception. Through Naaman's story I have come to see Your ways as compared to my ways. Holy Spirit, please reveal the offenses I have made toward God and myself because of my presumptions. Forgive me; I will address each one as You show them to me. I promise to let go and not make excuses for leaving them in my life. Cleanse me by the blood of Jesus. I'm ready for a closer walk with you. Help me not to condemn myself but to accept your conviction. You are Truth and Your Word is truth.

Thank you, Lord. I love you.

Gehazi Presumed on God's Timing

Chapter Three

"Is it time to receive…? (2 Kings 5:26).

Six years ago I daily searched the Internet for two weeks waiting on the price of flights from California to Georgia to go down. I wanted to book my vacation to visit my son, Carlton, his wife, Kisha, and my grandchildren in early August before his two older children went back to school and preschool.

My goal each year is to be with them at least twice a year. I pay for the low fare flight then use accumulated flight miles through American Express for a more expensive ticket. I was thrilled to see I had enough flight miles credit to book a round trip. I called Kisha, told her the good news. We agreed on the dates and that I would book my flight the next day.

That morning I thanked God it was time to see my grandkids. I prayed about the trip and asked God to work out all the details, and then I sat down at my computer. Suddenly I felt bad. You know that icky feeling which tells you something is not right. I try not to override this.

"Lord, are you saying I'm not to go to Atlanta in a couple of weeks? Is this not the time?"

There were no words spoken but that bad feeling got worse. If only we had something more to go on than the *gut feeling* that something just isn't right. When we experience that uneasy feeling, we need to stop right where we are and consult the Holy Spirit by asking one question at a time. Questions such as: Am I not to do this? If I am to do "this," is it for now? Is it for later? Is there another person you want me to talk to than the one I have in mind? Am I to do business with this person? If yes, is it for now? If no, am I to do business with a partner? Or start my business alone? Practice asking the Holy Spirit what to do to become aware of what He is saying. Ask Him to increase your capacity to hear from God.

I call this line of questioning of the Holy Spirit, "Lowest Common Denominator" questions, which requires a simple *yes* or *no* from Him.

I called Kisha and said, "The Holy Spirit is cautioning me that this is not the time to come. I'm so disappointed, but I don't want to presume. I'll ask God often until He lets me know His timing."

Kisha said, "Oh, I'm disappointed too. I know you really want to see your grandkids, but Mamma Diane I want to tell you something if it's OK. Your voice sounds like a little kid whose Dad just told her she cannot go out to play. It's kinda funny."

Carlton had received a promotion and was scheduled to start a new position with Kroger at corporate headquarters in Cincinnati, Ohio sometime after the first of the year. His family was going to relocate after the sale of their home in Georgia. Suddenly he received a call the beginning of November from his soon-to-be-boss.

"Mr. Hemphill, I have your contract in front of me. You start right after the first of the year in your new position. I know this will be sudden and inconvenient, but we will have key meetings before Thanksgiving and other end-of-the-year meetings in December. We need you here immediately to get you up to speed so you can hit the ground running in January.

"Everything in this contract will be done, only sooner: furnished apartment, rental car, we'll fly you home twice a month to be with your family and take care of the sale of your house, a ticket for your wife to fly to Ohio to buy a home here. I see here it also says we will pay a babysitter $300 to watch your children while your wife is in Ohio for a week. You will handle all the particulars through our relocation service coordinator, here is Nancy's number..."

Carlton called me after touching bases with Nancy, and excitedly shared all details with me.

"Mom, Kisha and I want you to fly here to keep the kids while we look for a house in Cincinnati. Kisha will take baby Christina with her. They gave me $300 toward my babysitter which we will use on your flight. We'll pray and find a way to pay for the total ticket. You need to be here the Friday after Thanksgiving and plan to stay for a week. I'm excited! The only down side is I will miss my family on Thanksgiving Day. In fact, it will be the first time in my life I will be by myself on Thanksgiving."

I responded, "Oh honey, I'm so excited for you! Yes, the Lord will show us how to make that happen. Let me move some things in my schedule and call you in a couple of days."

I prayed *Jesus, You are the administrator of all things so reveal the best way to administrate this trip by the Holy Spirit's leading.*

The light bulb came on and I knew what to do! I used my flight miles for the beginning of the trip and the $300 I applied to the one-way ticket from Atlanta back to California which cost $379. We applied the $300 and Carlton paid the $79.

I surprised Carlton and flew to Ohio Thanksgiving Eve (of course I told him before boarding the plane to meet me at the airport after work). We did a prayer drive (same as a prayer walk but in a car) as we drove through downtown Cincinnati. We prayed over his and Kisha's purpose in the region, the right home, schools, church, babysitters, and the right people connections. We ate at a nice restaurant and had a wonderful Thanksgiving Day together. Friday I flew to Atlanta, Kisha and Christina flew to Ohio on Saturday. I had a great time with Jeana, Little Carlton, and Kisha's younger sister, Krystal, who was visiting from Oklahoma and was a great help.

Timing is the ability to select the precise moment for doing something for optimum effect.

God knows the future, so even when we have made our plans and asked Him to bless them, check back with Him again and see if He has something further to say. He should have the last word.

He can give everyone involved the desires of their hearts simultaneously. The ticket from California to Ohio to Georgia was $1200. It only cost me $100 in fees. I gave up my timing in August to receive His time in November. Watching God work is awesome!

Patience and understanding are the keys to cooperating with God's timing. Gehazi didn't wait on God's timing nor seek understanding from Elisha. Instead he presumed they would get paid the normal way through the gifts of those seeking ministry. But it didn't happen. The Bible doesn't say why it was not time to receive finances for a job well done, but I have some thoughts on the subject that we will examine.

In January 1984 at an evangelistic training school in Anaheim, Dr. Morris Cerullo, a world-renowned evangelist, spoke profound words to the 7,000 in attendance.

"After decades of following the Lord, if I were going to reduce all I know about God's guidance to one word it would be *timing*."

From that time forward I started paying more attention to signs God gave that signified something was or was not in His timing. I worked to stop presuming on God's time table about when to start or stop something. Sometimes it's easier to know *what* God wants you to do than it is to know *when* God wants you to do it. I even stopped using the phrase "it must not have been God's timing" as an excuse when a prayer wasn't answered. Sometimes it may not have been His timing; other times I've used this phrase because I didn't want to go back to the Lord and continue seeking Him until I could get an understanding. That's a lot of work, but I teach people that this time spent checking back with the Holy Spirit can be the difference between having knowledge of what did or didn't happen, and having wisdom from the Holy Spirit as to why something did or didn't happen.

Elisha's long time faithful assistant, Gehazi, came under the judgment of God after Naaman's healing. It troubled me for years when I read this story as to why he was judged so severely. There had to be more to the story than simply his greed for some money and some clothes. Then I saw it! One phrase from Elisha I had overlooked for years—is it *time* to receive money and receive clothing...?

In Old Testament times, and even today, it's customary when you want ministry from a "Seer" or "Prophet" that you bring money, clothes, food, or some valuable treasure. The prophet's responsibility is to pray and know the voice of the Lord; in our day the Bible, and to go wherever the Lord needs him or her. Their livelihood, in this case and also the priests from the tribe of Levi, was supplied by the people who came to receive their services. The priests and the prophets received income for their ministry.

Today this principle applies to pastors, evangelists, Bible teachers, too. Much like we pay a consultant today. I have seen consultants spend two hours and walk away with thousands of dollars from a business. The payment was not just for the two hours spent; they are paid for the value added because of the consultant's years of study, preparation, and wisdom. The same should be for those in ministry today. Elisha and Gehazi were paid by the gifts they were given for their service and value added.

Naaman, leader of the Syrian army, had contracted leprosy while doing battle for the king of Syria. He heard there was a prophet, Elisha, in Israel who could pray for him to be healed. He went to the king to ask permission to go. The king gave him, clothes, silver, and gold to give the prophet.

And Elisha sent a messenger [Gehazi] *to him* [Naaman], *saying, "Go and wash in the Jordan seven times, and your flesh shall be restored to you, and you shall be clean"* (2 Kings 5:10). *And he* [Naaman] *returned to the man of God, he and all his aides, and came and stood before him; and he said, "Indeed, now I know that there is no God in all the earth, except in Israel; now therefore, please take a gift from your servant. But he* [Elisha] *said, "As the Lord lives, before whom I stand, I will receive nothing." And he* [Naaman] *urged him to take it, but he* [Elisha] *refused* (2 Kings 5:15-16).

Until this time, Gehazi had been a faithful servant to Elisha. He was instrumental in the raising of the Shunammite woman's dead son in 2 Kings 4:8-36. In a similar way as Elisha served Elijah, Gehazi was always by his side through every trial and every miraculous victory. Often he is only mentioned as the servant.

Gehazi watched this exchange of dialogue between Naaman and Elisha in amazement. Like we so often do when we anticipate getting paid for our work, we calculate in our head what we are going to do with our portion. After all Gehazi had done his part as always and felt he had earned his pay.

But Gehazi, the servant of Elisha the man of God, said, "Look, my master has spared Naaman this Syrian, while not receiving from his hands what he brought; but as the Lord lives, I will run after him and take something from him." So Gehazi pursued Naaman. When Naaman saw him running after him, he got down from the chariot to meet him, and said, "Is all well?"

And he said, "All is well. My master has sent me, saying, 'Indeed, just now two young men of the sons of the prophets have come to me from the mountains of Ephraim. Please give them a talent of silver and two changes of garments.'"

So Naaman said, "Please, take two talents." And he urged him, and bound two talents of silver in two bags, with two changes of garments, and handed them to two of his servants; and they carried them on ahead of him. When he came to the citadel, he took them from their hand, and stored them away in the house; then he let the men go, and they departed (2 Kings 5:21-24).

Gehazi left without getting an understanding from Elisha. Why didn't they receive payment for the work they did? I guess he forgot he was dealing with a perceptive prophet of God. Gehazi certainly presumed he could hide his wrongdoing from the prophet who was sensitive to God's voice.

Now he went in and stood before his master. Elisha said to him, "Where did you go, Gehazi?"

And he said, "Your servant did not go anywhere."

Then he said to him, "Did not my heart go with you when the man turned back from his chariot to meet you? Is it time to receive money and to receive clothing, olive groves and vineyards, sheep and oxen, male and female servants? Therefore the leprosy of Naaman shall cling to you and your descendants forever." And he went out from his presence leprous, as white as snow (2 Kings 5:25-27).

How eerie that story is. God didn't heal Naaman so He could put the disease on Gehazi. That is not God's nature. Gehazi opened the door to his own judgment by his actions.

The level of your God-given influence will be the level of your humiliation when you fall. Gehazi had a unique privileged responsibility before God and man.

As I read the story of Gehazi again I could hear his plight. I believe it was more than greed but an understandable presumption and expectation of finances based on what was customary. But he refused to submit to the one in authority and learn why this time Elisha refused. He may have learned something about the timing-of-the-Lord.

I have responsibility for a group of people. So even on vacation or away ministering God has sometimes given me a dream or vision of someone in my congregation or family who had done something wrong. Like Elisha I felt "my heart go with them" into that dark place and I prayed for their recovery. I knew what happened and what they had done—not all the details, but enough to know the basics. We would meet together when I returned and God would show me whether to give mercy or judgment according to their maturity and their heart attitude.

These key words which Elisha said are what made this time different, "Is it *time* to receive...?"

God did *not* want Naaman, a person of great pride, to feel as though he in any way "bought" his miracle. I also believe God wanted to send a message to the enemy of Israel, the king of Syria. God may have wanted to amaze him that there was no "gift" taken for their service. God's goodness softens hearts. Therefore, this could have touched the king's heart in a way that would cause his heart to turn favorably to Israel. Even to them becoming allies. Whatever the outcome intended, God had a specific purpose that went beyond Elisha and Gehazi's personal needs.

Is it time to receive? There's a time to give and a time to receive, a time to refrain from giving and a time to refrain from receiving. God's kingdom economics dictates the *time* not our personal needs.

Gehazi should have waited a moment and moved past his presumption and greed and questioned Elisha. He was not a novice. He could have learned a major key about God's timing. Instead he poisoned God's timing in a major way and suffered the consequences.

This reminds me of an incident with my worship leader at my church, Kecia Lewis. Kecia sang professionally in New York on Broadway for years before moving to California where she became my worship leader.

In August 1997, I took a team of seven women to New Zealand to host four of my Beautiful Women of God Seminars in four regions on the North Island. I took two New Zealanders who were living in America and five Americans. One New Zealander was my Assistant Pastor, Diane Bowater.

We ministered at churches on Sundays and did my Beautiful Women of God seminars Thursday through Saturday. God wonderfully healed and blessed countless people. On our schedule was a vibrant church we were going to visit but we were not scheduled to minister there.

Encounter Church, pastored by Senior Leaders Brent and Patricia Douglas, had a vibrant music ministry which produced praise and worship CDs with original songs. Churches throughout the entire nation purchased their CDS and sang their songs.

As God would have it, Encounter was producing a CD project the weekend we planned to visit them. Rev. Diane Bowater was a friend to the Douglases, shared with them we were planning to visit on that particular Sunday.

Six months earlier on my first trip to New Zealand I brought home music from that country. One of our favorite songs from there was one of their original songs. We added hand movements for fun. We sang it regularly in our church in Riverside, California.

Rev. Bowater said, "Pastor Diane Gardner is a powerfully anointed speaker, you should think about having her speak and minister to your people. At my church in Riverside our worship leader is a professional singer with an outstanding voice range so we sing your song 'Jump in the Water' better than you guys do."

I was a bit embarrassed when I heard how she approached them. Nevertheless, they were excited because they were planning to do a remix of that popular song on their new project.

Pastor Brent Douglas contacted me and discussed my speaking in their morning service. He said Pastor Patricia was in charge of the music project being done at the evening service and they wanted Kecia to sing two songs. He gave me the details and we made an appointment to sign the legal papers for Kecia's services on the Monday morning following the project.

I spoke in the morning service which went extremely well. They gave me a speaker honorarium and took up an offering for expenses for my team. We were grateful for the unexpected financial blessings. It was a time for my team and me to receive. That evening we sang on their live recording, which was powerful. The non singers' microphones, including mine, were on low volume. They wanted the hand movements we had added to the song for their congregation to learn. And it looked good to have all of us participating. Kecia sang lead on "Jump in the Water" and also sang a spontaneous original worship song.

Monday morning Kecia and I entered their music headquarters, which was in a separate building from the church.

Senior Leader Brent Douglas said, "Hello, good job yesterday, Kecia, you were spot on! Patricia and I could not be more pleased! You have an awesome voice!"

He led us a few steps to a couple of beautiful navy blue overstuffed chairs. Our hearts were overjoyed. We couldn't stop smiling.

Pastor Patricia, the creator of the music project said to Kecia, "Here is a paper for your mailing address and basic information. I'll give you the contract and we will go over the few blank spaces and I'll explain the rest as soon as you finish this one."

She handed Kecia a paper. Then she said, "We are excited to offer you royalties on the two songs you lead. We haven't a clue what it will add up to, but we know in the next few months this will be throughout the nation. We will send your royalty checks quarterly directly to your address you just wrote down."

Kecia scooted to the edge of her chair and said, "Thank you Pastors, I…"

I reached over and squeezed her left knee really tight to interrupt her.

"Pastor Patricia thanks so much but Kecia will not be receiving any royalties from this project." I became stern in my voice as Kecia turned to stare intently at me. I caught a glimpse of her from the corner of my eye.

Senior Leader Pastor Brent stood up and took a step closer to our chairs. Pastor Patricia dropped her arm to her side with the contract in her hand.

I continued to carry the conversation, "It is not *time* for Kecia to receive money for a Gospel project. This is her first fruit offering. It has been a dream of Kecia's to produce her own Gospel CD. This is her first experience singing on a Gospel CD project, so she will *invest* these royalties back into the soil of this project.

"In exchange we ask that you and your staff pray for Kecia for an open door to produce her own CD when it's time. We invest this money large or small, and we choose prayer covering as our return on our investment, or rather Kecia's investment."

My right hand was still on Kecia's left knee and I felt her leg begin to quiver. I gave a quick glance at her with a smile and I could tell she was holding her breath.

Pastor Brent asked as he looked at Kecia, "Are you absolutely *sure* that's all you want from us?"

Kecia nodded her head. Speechless and with half a smile she gave her consent.

"Well, we were not expecting that," Pastor Patricia said, "So let's pray now."

They prayed beautifully over Kecia concerning where God would lead her to touch lives through her future Gospel projects.

Kecia signed the contract indicating she would not receive any money on the sale of these CDs.

We hugged each other and left the building.

After I got in the car Kecia came and knocked on my window. I let the window down.

"I just need to say, even through my clinched teeth, that I trust you. If you say it isn't *time* to receive royalties then I submit to that. However, I don't fully understand. Although I want to, so I know we will talk when we get back to the States." She sighed deeply a couple of times.

Then she continued, "For my own anxiety level to go down, I need to say this. I know you remember that I have no money of my own at this stage in my life. My mother and her best friend sold BBQ dinners and asked her friends to donate. She totally sponsored this ministry trip for me. You also remember I am working and living at the unwed mothers' home in Long Beach, and the donors have not been giving to the home lately. So for months now I have been without a salary. And you still said it is *not time to receive* any royalties."

She paused and with a fake grin said, "I'm smiling so the others don't know I'm going crazy right now. But it will be OK. I know you hear from God clearly and have my best interest at heart."

I responded, "We will talk back home. I am overjoyed at what you've just done. You have set yourself up for a miracle! God loves a cheerful giver. This is an investment you will be happy about in days to come! This is the beginning of your dream!" I patted her on the back of her right hand resting on the open window of the car door. "Trust God and trust me and you'll see."

Although it may have been tempting, I'm thankful Kecia did not do like Gehazi and mess up God's economic plan out of greed or impatience.

Exactly one year later, she auditioned for *The Sound of Music* to play the Mother Superior at the Santa

Barbara Theatre. She got the part. She won awards and was offered the opportunity to produce her own Christmas Gospel special. I have a picture of her standing in front of the theatre with the marquee that says: Kecia Lewis Christmas Concert Sold Out! The auditorium seated close to a thousand. My dance team danced, my worship team sang and played as Kecia's back up. Our friends, Pastors John and Dana Roman, played the piano and sang. We could not have been more ecstatic. At the performance, through the director, God opened the door for me to give a short prayer of salvation for those who wanted to become born again. God is truly miraculous!

That's not all! While performing with *The Sound of Music* Kecia asked the director of the theatre, a wonderful Christian man, if she could seek sponsors for her first Gospel music project. The director said, "Kecia, I cannot let you announce something like that from the platform, but if you bring me a flyer I will approve for you to have as many as you want in the foyer.

She did and received a few phone calls. Then one day she received a call from an American lawyer for a foreign country. He did not know the Lord, and was not interested in the Gospel, but loved Kecia's voice. He said he was looking for his next investment project and this sounded like a fun investment.

He singlehandedly financed two Gospel CD projects, and also totally financed Kecia's salary for three years. He paid for her entertainment lawyer, publicist, agent, producer, musicians, studio time, debut concerts, and all airfare for each television appearance. Telling about it again stirs my heart and brings tears of gratitude to the Lord and for the financier. Toward the end of the three year project I stood next to him as we watched Kecia rehearse for her concert.

"Rev. Diane this has been so much fun for me and interesting. I've never been a part of this world you guys live in. I still enjoy watching her sing, she truly is special. This has cost me way more than I was planning. So far I have spent $300,000 investing in her and I don't regret a dime. Thank you for being our spiritual leader to help things stay on track."

He is such a quality man. We shared the gospel numerous times with him, but he kept saying he didn't want to make that kind of commitment. I'm still praying for him.

Gehazi missed his blessing through presumption, impatience, greed, and lack of submission to God's appointed one in authority, Elisha. Kecia did not miss her opportunity. She released her presumption, did not choose greed, but chose patience, submitted her plans and desires to God and His appointed one in authority, me.

Here's a Scripture to meditate on that Kecia asked me to share with you. This is where she has found wisdom when looking for God's timetable. It helps her know when to sacrifice, when to give, and when to reap a harvest.

Proverbs 13:10 AMP shows us when it comes to God's purpose we don't' have to walk alone.

Through pride and presumption come nothing but strife, But [skillful and godly] wisdom is with those who welcome [well-advised] counsel.

Everyone who has an opinion of what you should do is not that "well-advised" counsel. Ask God to show you who He has assigned for this season in your life. It may be someone else for another season. Don't hang onto someone just because they were used in the past.

You may not receive financing to the tune of $300,000, but you *will* certainly reap your rewards whether monetary or in other ways. You'll see your rewards if you begin to care more about God's economy. Seek His challenging ways rather than your easy ways and choose to become patient.

I have made it a practice to give a good portion or all of my first fruits of any increase back to the Lord as an investment to increase. I always discuss with Him what I am investing it for.

Honor the Lord with your capital and sufficiency [from righteous labors] and with the firstfruits of all your income; So shall your storage places be filled with plenty, and your vats shall be overflowing with new wine (Proverbs 3:9-10 AMP).

Seek God, not the end result of money, fame, fortune, position, and people. Seek the Giver rather than His gifts.

Hebrews 11:6 NIV says: *And without faith it is impossible to please God, because anyone who comes to him must believe that he exists and that he rewards those who earnestly seek Him.*

NKJV says it this way: But without faith it is impossible to please Him, for he who comes to God must believe that He is, and that He is a rewarder of those who diligently seek Him.

He is a rewarder so you will get the gifts. But you must allow Him to reward you His way in His *timing*.

Faith: Foundation for Hope

Chapter Four

Now faith is the assurance of things hoped for, the conviction of things not seen. For by it the people of old received their commendation. By faith we understand that the universe was created by the word of God, so that what is seen was not made out of things that are visible (Hebrews 11:1-3 ESV).

"I sure hope so." I'm sure you've heard this phrase thousands of times. You've probably said it yourself a time or two. It is an expression many people use. It can be a statement of faith, the mindset behind the word hope, or an empty phrase full of doubt? More often than not it is the latter. We want to use our faith, but we are often afraid to really "get our hopes up." However, we cannot develop faith and have empty hope.

The definitions for the word hope are broad and range from a wish or desire for something to somebody who has a feeling of trust. We use the word hope like a vague wish before we blow out our birthday candles or we use it to express the greatest definition for Christians, which is Christ in you the hope of glory.

Against hope Abraham, the father of our faith, believed in hope. That sounds like double talk. Against hope—believed in hope? This actually became an exciting Scripture when I finally got it.
Romans 4:17-19 says of Abraham: *as it is written, "I have made you a father of many nations" in the presence of Him whom he believed—God, who gives life to the dead and calls those things which do not exist as though they did; who, contrary to hope, in hope believed, so that he became the father of many nations, according to what was spoken, "So shall your descendants be." And not being weak in faith, he did not consider his own body, already dead (since he was about a hundred years old), and the deadness of Sarah's womb.*

The Message (MSG) Bible shares Romans 4:17-19 this way: We call Abraham "father" not because he got God's attention by living like a saint, but because God made something out of Abraham when he was a nobody. Isn't that what we've always read in Scripture, God saying to Abraham, "I set you up as father of many peoples?" Abraham was first named "father" and then became a father because he dared to trust God to do what only God could do: raise the dead to life, with a word make something out of nothing. When everything was hopeless, Abraham believed anyway, deciding to live not on the basis of what he saw he couldn't do but on what God said he would do. And so he was made father of a multitude of peoples. God himself said to him, "You're going to have a big family, Abraham!"

Against all natural hope—a formless empty wish— Abraham had hope in God. This gave him a specific direction of trust, creating a form or boundaries for his faith.

We can't be filled with faith until we first have hope in a specific expectation. The understanding of this truth came to me clearly years ago when I helped my husband lay concrete to extend our driveway.

The first thing we did was to get an idea or vision of the final foundation; we discussed different ideas until our vision was the same for the final dimensions: height, depth, width, and shape when finished. For this project we chose a rectangular shape for the form. We had a specific vision of the outcome. That's how we knew what shape to make it. Next, we made our form from solid wood boards. Without the form (solid boundaries) the concrete had no idea what it was to look like after it was poured. Without a set form concrete will run in every direction at once and when hardened it will look like a horrible formless mess.

We mixed the dry concrete and smashed all the lumps. The next most important ingredient we added was water. A sufficient amount of water was poured while mixing the concrete until the desired consistency was reached. I'd seen this done, but this was my first time being an active participant. Actually, I was a little impatient with the mixing and pouring water process. I kept asking, "Is it ready yet?" And I was told "Not yet." Until I finally decided the only way to enjoy this process was to use patience.

Finally, it was the right consistency. We poured it into the form slowly, the concrete piled up in the middle, and we had shovels to push it to its edges. Soon the concrete knew exactly what shape it was to take and what its parameters were. We spread everything using our nice trowel as our best tool. Afterwards we used patience to wait on the concrete to do its work and become a solid foundation. After it dried completely we could stand on it with no problem and even park our car on it with no worries. It is still a solid useful foundation today.

It's our time to produce for the King and His Kingdom. So as His leaders for this generation let's build a legacy of faith that will last for succeeding generations. Hope is our form. If our hope is formless, our faith, like our concrete, will not know what is expected of it. So we must be specific in forming our hope and base it on:

God's promises in His Word.

His nature as a good, merciful and loving Father.

What the Holy Spirit is revealing right now about our current situation.

Let's clearly form our frame of hope.

When we make a decision to apply our faith to a specific thing, we must mix it with water (Holy Spirit) for it to become pliable to the Will of God. We do this by inviting Him to guide us and be in the "mix." The concrete mix cannot become what it is designed to be without water. It's the same way for us: hope (form), faith (concrete), and Holy Spirit (water) together equal a firm foundation that lasts for generations.

There are many symbols in the Bible that reflect the Holy Spirit and His work. Water is one of those symbols or types (representations). One of my favorite passages on this is when Jesus talked to the Samaritan woman at the well in John 4:14 says: *But whoever drinks of the water that I shall give him will never thirst. But the water that I shall give him will become in him a fountain of water springing up into everlasting life.*

Notice the comparison to water as a type of the Holy Spirit. Another much loved passage is found in John 7:38-39: *He who believes in Me, as the Scripture has said, out of his heart will flow rivers of living water. But this He spoke concerning the Spirit, whom those believing in Him would receive; for the Holy Spirit was not yet given, because Jesus was not yet glorified.*

After mixing the water of the Spirit, then we pour our faith (cement) into the hope we have formed. Next we exercise our patience for the faith to harden and become the firm foundation on which we can stand.

Faith becomes the substance of the things we hope for. I can see this picture in my mind's eye now. Presumption on the other hand is like forming the frame of hope, then pouring nothing in but our thoughts. When we stand on that foundation we don't have "a leg to stand on." What we had hoped to be firm and solid is empty.

Not long after I heard my first sermon on presumption I sought understanding on what was the difference between my hope, faith, and presumption. This circumstance opened my eyes to a new world of understanding. I have never forgotten the lesson I learned from a story that comes to mind of my son Curtis when he was five-years-old.

"Curtis, why are your toes sticking out of the top of your new shoe? Your sock and your shoe are completely gone! Come here, Son," I motioned to him. "Let me see your shoe. I've never seen the top of a new pair of shoes wear out like this, and the bottom still looks new. Last week your dad polished them because I showed him how the top of your right shoe was badly scuffed up. Do you know how you got a hole in your shoe and sock?"

Before he could answer, my mind started racing. *Oh no! This is his only pair of shoes he has and I don't have money to buy new ones. Tomorrow is church, and Monday starts school. What am I going to do?*

He responded with a sense of achievement. "Mom, I stopped the merry-go-round with the top of my shoe. I put my leg out like this." He extended his right leg out to the side, and then put the top of his shoe on the floor. Noticing the worried look on my face he looked down sheepishly with his head cocked to one side, as he tried to justify his actions.

"I can stop it better with the top of my shoe instead of the bottom."

It was a childish mistake, and I didn't want to be too hard on him. I took a deep breath and said. "OK, Son, let's pray and ask Jesus for another pair of shoes. We held hands and prayed, "Lord Jesus, Your Word says to ask You. In Mark 11:24, Jesus You told us, *Therefore I say to you, whatever things you ask when you pray, believe that you receive them, and you will have them.* We ask you for new shoes. And now we thank you for shoes for Curtis to wear to church tomorrow and to school next week. I receive them now. We praise Your name."

The next day Curtis wore his house slippers to church. Twice he put his feet up on the back of the pew in front of him. I was totally embarrassed my child had no "real" shoes on. I quickly pushed his feet down both times. Suddenly I had a brilliant idea. God is going to use this to show the people behind us that Curtis has on slippers. They will pray and ask God how they can help this poor child, and God will tell them to buy him some "real" shoes for school. We'll shop after lunch today, and I'll give the testimony tonight at the evening service.

So the next time he put his feet on the back of the pew, I left them there and took a quick glance to the right then to the left behind us to see who was sitting on the row behind us.

I hung around church until the last persons left. Nothing happened. I returned home deeply disappointed and on the verge of tears. While the kids and their dad napped after lunch I had another brilliant idea.

It didn't happen this morning because I think surely someone will see his slippers tonight and put money in my hand, and we'll have time to run to the store before they close so my family won't be embarrassed to send him to school in slippers.

Again, I kept Curtis close to me so adults could be sure and see him. Again we were the last to leave. Absolutely nothing happened. No money, no shoes, no testimony of God's goodness. My presumption led me to be angry all evening.

In the morning I expressed my disappointment and anger to God. I didn't pray. I only complained, and I got no response from Him.

Curtis wore slippers to school all week. One day I felt angry and the next day I shed tears of despair as Curtis walked out the door for school. At the end of the week my husband received is paycheck from his job and we purchased shoes and socks on Saturday. I was somewhat relieved the shoe situation was resolved, but also disgusted Curtis had worn his slippers for a week. I felt my flesh being crucified all week.

The following week I finally talked to God about this from a heart of humility seeking truth. I wanted to understand what went wrong. "God, did you hear my prayer? Why did I have to be embarrassed at church and Curtis had to be embarrassed at school the rest of the week? Didn't I pray in faith like you wanted?" I paused when I realized I had asked three questions at once, and I needed to slow down and ask one at a time. "Uh, I know I asked a lot of questions at once. So I'll backtrack and ask one question at a time." I did.

Through His grace and because I finally had a heart to seek truth beyond my feelings of frustration, the Holy Spirit gently corrected me and brought understanding. My hope was right because I had an expectation that God would answer our prayer for shoes. I discovered I had prayed in faith according to His Will. He revealed I also prayed according to His Word. This pleased God just as Hebrews 11:6a states: *But without faith it is impossible to please Him, for he who comes to God must believe that He is, and that He is a rewarder of those who diligently seek Him.*

Unfortunately, I added my presumption to the faith equation. God and I agreed on what needed to be taken care of: new shoes for Curtis. God never said nor agreed with me on the when, where, how and through whom He was going to answer my reasonable request. I added those details.

I was shocked when God revealed to me that embarrassment is rooted in pride. To feel embarrassed is normal, but the Holy Spirit challenged me to learn to quickly let go of embarrassment and not make decisions because of it. If I allow embarrassment to rear its ugly head I will blame someone else for how I feel, justify my actions, or completely shut down.

I heard Him say, *don't let embarrassment rob you of My highest and best. You will be tempted to pre-serve your pride and not move forward to what I have for you to say or do.* WOW!

That revelation rocked my world. I saw where I could have overly corrected my son each day when I felt the embarrassment as I sent him to school. He could have gone to school with an emotional cloud of condemnation daily if I was trying to get the embarrassment off me and put it on him or at least have him feel as bad as I did. Thank God I didn't do that.

From then on I became keenly aware how often parents overly correct their children in the grocery store, at restaurants, at church, or wherever their child does something to embarrass them.

Finally, I realized He answered my prayer through our regular paycheck from the job God had already supplied. It's no less of a "gift" from God when it comes through our earnings than if someone hands us money unexpectedly, although the latter does feel more exciting.

Living by faith and expecting God to answer our prayers in essential to our relationship with Him. However, presuming the details of those answered prayers can be costly because unresolved it can lead to bitterness and resentment toward God.

Let's pray.

Father, I see now the subtle way my presuming can interfere with our relationship.

Forgive me for presuming on You, especially in this
_____ situation.

Cleanse me by the blood of Jesus. I take respon-sibility for my presumptive thinking. Let it not have dominion over me. I forgive myself also for my unrealistic expectations. As I read this book, I trust the Holy Spirit does a mighty work in me. Amen.

The Five Ws and One H of Presumption: Who, What, When, Where, Why, and How

Chapter Five

For My thoughts are not your thoughts, Nor are your ways My ways, says the Lord.
For as the heavens are higher than the earth, so are My ways higher than your ways,
And My thoughts than your thoughts (Isaiah 55:8-9).

When I was eight years old a doctor told my Mom I was under weight for my height. Until then I was a happy picky eater and she didn't care. Now she equated my thin, underweight body with being unhealthy. The doctor never said I was unhealthy.

But this being the late 1950s and my Mom, who was from Texas, determined to put "meat on my bones," which was a popular saying from the Southern US back in the day.

From that time forward I could not leave the table until my plate was clean. She let me know she was increasing my capacity to receive more food. Every week I had to eat more than the last week. By the time I was twelve I could keep pace with my Dad when it came to meals. As a teenager when I had a date for dinner I ate a full meal before I left our house, so my date didn't see how much I could eat. Also I wasn't sure if he could afford to feed me.

In the same way Mom devised a plan for increase, we must be intentional about increasing our capacity to hear from God. Guidance from the Lord can be filled with uncertainty, seem confusing, and challenges our comfort zone. The increase of our capacity to hear from God won't happen by accident, osmosis, or hoping so. It only happens deliberately and intentionally.

What might limit our capacity to hear and receive from God? It could be presumptions, unscriptural traditions, superstitions, anxiety, worry, fear, rebellion, stubbornness, pride, lack of knowledge, etc. Each one can take up space where truth should reside.

God will never fill a place which is already occupied. Neither will He kick out something that shouldn't be there. A glass full of water has no capacity to receive anything else. We must expand our capacity and make more space by emptying our "glasses." That's our job, with the Holy Spirit's help, not God's job. We are to empty ourselves of our "stinking thinking"—one wrong belief at a time. Our Helper, the Holy Spirit knows everything we need to empty and everything the Father wants us to have. Just ask Him.

We are on a search for truth. We can approach getting to the truth the same way a prosecuting attorney prepares for court, a journalist prepares to write a documentary, and a high school teacher prepares his or her students to write a story. They all follow the same principle rule of thumb to present the true facts. Often they use what is commonly called "The Five Ws and One H" or "The Kipling Method."

Rudyard Kipling, an author of adult and children's books, and a poet, shared this principle which did not originate with him, but he gave it poetry and made the Five Ws and One H memorable:

I keep six honest serving-men
(They taught me all I knew);
Their names are **W**hat and **W**hy and **W**hen
And **H**ow and **W**here and **W**ho.

DIANE GARDNER

The same principle of the six basic questions is what we will use to go on our fact-finding mission when we seek God for answers. In other words these are the questions that must be answered in order to get to the bottom of the truth.

Gathering answers to these six basic questions can help us to proceed more quickly and smoothly as we seek direction. If we want guidance that is accurate then we need answers from God's thoughts, not ours or anyone else's, on as many of these six questions as possible. God can use anyone He wants to give us some of our answers so we ask Him and refrain from asking the people around us.

When we don't have answers for all six, any from God puts us on the right track if we resist the temptation to *add* our thoughts to the truth God shared. If God shares the what, where, who, then we must resist the temptation to make it into a neat little package we can wrap up and be done with. We must not add the when, why, and how. We might have heard *accurately* from the Lord and then *added* our presumptions to His truth to fill in the blanks. The result may still have an outcome God never intended.

What is it that God wants me to do?

68

Why does God want me to do it? (This relates to the purpose on His mind. This is not asking *Why* out of whining, complaining, or doubt)

When does God want me to start and when does He want me to be finished?

Where does God want this to take place?

Who is the person God wants to work through? Who am I to connect with? Who doesn't He want me to connect with?

How is this going to take place? How is the door going to open, the money going to come, I'm going to purchase that property, start that ministry?

Seeking guidance from God requires us to ask specific questions if we want specific answers. Our thoughts are limited and the Lord is Omniscient (all knowing). He also sees the motives of our heart.

All the ways of a man are clean and innocent in his own eyes [and he may see nothing wrong with his actions]. But the Lord weighs and examines the motives and intents [of the heart and knows the truth] (Proverbs 16:2 AMP)

There was an important circumstance that happened where I sought God diligently. I received His answer to What, When, Where, Who, but not Why, and How. Because I had enough of the Five Ws and One H to move forward I did. The entire time I was *on track* with God but it didn't look like it. At the end of ten months I came to Him in desperation because I presumed I must have missed Him. I went back over the question I believed I had heard answers to and allowed Him to confirm or deny what He had said or not said. Then He answered the last two questions and I understood. Here's what happened.

As a part of my divorce agreement with my former husband of twenty-four years, our house was to be sold the year our son Carlton graduated from college. We presumed this to be less than two years after our divorce began. Our oldest son Curtis was married and lived on his own. As a result we refinanced the home we had lived in for fifteen years while pulling out every bit of allowable equity. We divided it between us and some expenses for Carlton in college. I put the majority of my money back into the house that was in desperate need of repairs. Our original plan when the house sold was for us to divide the small amount of equity if there were any left after expenses. Either way the house was to be sold.

Only about 100 days after he filed for divorce and during the California mandatory six months waiting period from the filing of a divorce until it is final, a tragedy happened. Carlton was at a party after Eastern Oregon States' first football scrimmage game; he hit his head on the sidewalk and sustained a major head injury.

After two weeks in intensive care the doctors said there was nothing more they could do for him. His brain was swollen and it was going to take months for the swelling to go down. After eighteen months whatever limitations he had at that time would be what he would live with for the rest of his life.

Carlton had to be watched 24/7. He absolutely could not sustain another head injury or it could cause death or put him in a vegetative state. He could never play football again (he had been recruited and received a partial football scholarship). I was told he could never return to college because of his inability to retain information. The hospital sent him home to me for him to recover.

Carlton was a twenty-one-year-old young man who acted like an elderly dementia patient with almost no short-term memory. I tell his full story in *Overcoming the Enemy's Storms* in the chapter titled *The Accident*. Needless to say this changed things for me. We had agreed for the house to go on the market in two years. Carlton certainly was not going to be graduating in another two years. I didn't mention anything about the house at the time; I simply presumed he felt the same way.

One year later while Carlton was still recovering from his head injury I received a call from Chuck, my former husband.

"Diane, it's time for you to get the house ready to be put on the market. If you start now then it will be sold before the year is out and we can have our money." He said with sternness in his voice.

"You're right, under normal circumstance that's what I would do. But Carlton as you know is still recovering and I'm running a ministry. We are still under the eighteen months recovery time for Carlton. I didn't want to have the pressure of a move while this is still going on with him. So I'm not going to put the house on the market just yet. Maybe in a couple of years when we see were Carlton is going to be by then. Let me know in a few weeks what you think."

He didn't see things that way. He accused me of trying to steal the rest of his equity. He came up with an amount which he determined I owed. The market did not support his theory. I mailed him some real estate comparisons for the area which showed the economy had absorbed the small amount of equity left after our refinance.

I said, "I'll put the house on the market when the value goes up. Right now we are upside down. Besides Carlton takes a lot of time to care for, even with no more things needed medically speaking. But he doesn't make sense all the time when he talks so it takes a while to decipher what he wants. He's much better but I need to watch him to make sure he doesn't walk out the door. The other day he put the microwave on 30 minutes instead of 3 minutes and set off the smoke alarm. I don't want the pressure of selling and moving right now. Did you receive the comps I sent from the real estate agent so you could see houses have gone down since you moved? Besides the house next door has gone into foreclosure and that affects our value."

Chuck replied, "I don't believe you. I saw what you sent me, but I don't care. You owe me $13,000 worth of equity. So get a loan and pay me what you owe me. Take out a second on the house. Do whatever it takes."

I took his suggestion to bring peace, but I couldn't qualify for a second on the house.

I called Chuck and said, "I told you I would take out the second but they said I didn't qualify. I don't make enough money to sustain the loan. We'll have to wait until the market picks up."

Chuck said, "No. That will not work for me. I already have a judge I have spoken to and he's going to suggest a lawyer to take you to court!"

"Chuck, I've done all I know to do, so you do what you want. Any judge with common sense will see there is no equity to withdraw."

After a couple of similar phone calls over the next couple of months I went to the Lord to seek wisdom on how to resolve this situation.

I got out three sheets of paper. I wrote out the Five Ws and One H, two per side with lots of space in between for me to write God's response or at least what I sensed at the time. I reduced my questions to their lowest common denominator (simplest form).

"Lord, is he going to let go of this accusation?" I sensed the answer was no.

"I think the answer is no to him letting go. Lord, what do you want me to do?"

Put the house up for sale now. I clearly heard this statement.

"Lord, You know how hard it will be to find a place to move let alone the actual move with everything concerning Carlton and my job. But like Peter said, 'Nevertheless at Your Word...' I will obey You and get the house ready to go on the market. Lead me to the agent right away. I'm not looking forward to this, but I trust You with the details."

I immediately took action presuming God would work some kind of miracle for us to receive a little money from the house. Ten months and two agents later I did not receive one offer on the house—even after reducing the price to below market value.

At this point, frustrated and weary, I checked back with the Lord to see if I could take the house off the market.

"Lord, Carlton and I are tired of living in a fishbowl every day because we don't know when someone will want to see the house. It hasn't sold, so can I take it off the market for now?"

God's response, *Yes.*

"But Lord, I was sure you told me to put the house on the market, but it didn't sell."

The Lord, answered, *Yes I told you to list the house, but I never said it would sell.*

I was shocked at that statement and asked, "God, I presumed if You wanted me to list the house You were going to sell the house. But you didn't. So why did You want me to list the house?"

God expressed, *You asked me what would silence Chuck about taking you to court. My response was for you to put the house up for sale. Chuck thought you were trying to steal the house from him so when you put it on the market and sent him a copy of the paperwork he was satisfied. He hasn't said anything to you about court, and when you told him it didn't sell he didn't threaten you anymore.*

I was surprised at the Lord's answer. I never thought of it in that way.

Amazed by God's technique in answering my prayers, "So Your *purpose* was never to sell the house? Your ways are certainly not my ways and they are always higher than my ways, so I guess I'm not moving to the cute apartment I found with the exercise room, business center and clubhouse. Oh, well. What do you want me to do now?"

God said, *I will tell you later when to sell your home.*

Three years later, after Carlton graduated and moved to Georgia for his job, God spoke to me clearly, *The house will sell this year.*

I was cleaning out stuff, removing wallpaper, and preparing the house to be put on the market, when I received a certified letter in the mail from Chuck. I thought *Oh no, my sons must have told him I was preparing the house to sell. I told them I was going to call him and send him a copy of the contract as soon as I got an agent.*

The letter read:

Diane, I'm writing to you about the house. You have owed me $13,000 for several years. I haven't mentioned this in a long time. With compounded interest, you now owe me $26,000.

I have been in a foreign country preparing to minister, and the Lord has been dealing with me a lot about this subject.

Under the direction of the Holy Spirit's instruction, I now release you of the **debt**. Whenever you sell the house you owe me nothing.

I know God will bless me for my obedience.

Sincerely,
Chuck

I was shocked. I read the note twice then put my reading glasses to see if there was any fine print. I held to letter up toward heaven and with tears streaming down my face I thanked the Lord for dealing with His son so profoundly. I shouted, "Debt cancellation!"

The house sold on December 31st. I opened a small IRA and put the majority of the money into upgrading my church building. Over the years the Lord has supernaturally financially sustained me while in fulltime ministry.

After a season of struggle, around ten years later Chuck did receive his reward for his obedience. Someone handed him $30,000 for a down payment on a house. I rejoiced with him when he mentioned how he received the down payment on the home he and his wife live in.

These are the steps I followed:
- **What**: I was to put the house on the market. I heard clearly from the Lord so I knew I was full of faith.
- **Why**: For the house to sell was my presumption. The Lord's truth was to change Chuck's heart and eventually have him cancel the debt.

- **When**: I was to put the house on the market immediately. I obeyed in faith.
- **Where**: The location was at my home, but I presumed I'd move to an apartment. The pressure to move while Carlton was recovering was never an issue with the Lord's plan because I didn't need to move during that time. Carlton moved before I did.
- **Who**: I never imagined Chuck would be who God would use.
- **How:** Chuck releasing me from any accountability to him concerning the sale of the house.

The Lord was clear in His instructions, and I obeyed those, but I added to them my common sense projections. He told me to put the house on the market not so it could sell but that will silence Chuck's threats.

The Five Ws and One H are crucial in receiving our guidance from the Holy Spirit. It is important to seek God to answer each of the Five Ws to move forward with His guidance. Don't panic if He is silent on some of them because sometimes He will show you what's missing later.

Be careful to understand what question God is answering with His response. If you ask several questions at once and God answers "yes," which question did He answer? To ensure you get the appropriate answer to each question ask one question and wait a few minutes for God's answer. Look at how you feel, not in your head, but go with your "gut feeling." Keep asking God a question and wait a few minutes for an answer to confirm each question's answer. Then trust Him that He has heard you and may answer you later while you are doing a "no brainer activity," such as driving, doing the dishes, sleeping, reading, walking, etc. Keep a notepad or record your thoughts on your phone, iPad, etc. The Holy Spirit will distinguish between your thoughts and God's thoughts. His thoughts are smarter, more humbling, more forgiving, more intelligent, and more loving than ours usually are.

You can pray this:
Father God, I recognize the importance of allowing You to show me the truth. I choose to empty my mind from the presumptions, pride, rebellion, stubbornness, traditions and superstations that fill my thinking. One by one I give you permission to reveal to me these counterfeits. I renounce their hold on me! Your ways are not my ways, Your ways are higher.

Your Word says in Isaiah 1:18-20
"Come now, and let us reason together," Says the Lord, "Though your sins are like scarlet,

They shall be as white as snow; Though they are red like crimson, They shall be as wool. If you are willing and obedient, You shall eat the good of the land; But if you refuse and rebel, You shall be devoured by the sword"; For the mouth of the Lord has spoken.

Thank You that You are a Father who wants to reason with me. I make the decision to be willing and obedient so I can eat the good of the land and receive my reward.

I ask You to help me increase my capacity to hear, understand, and act upon truth. I will take time to write down the Five Ws and One H when seeking guidance. I will exercise patience when I have heard part and not all the answers I need. I will resist the temptation to add my presumptions to Your truth.

With Your help I will surrender each situation to You and ask very specific questions; lowest common denominator questions so I can receive specific answers. Thank You for teaching me to apply this principle of The Five Ws and One H in my walk with You.

The Deadliest Presumption

Chapter Six

No one has gone up into heaven, but there is One who came down from heaven, the Son of Man [Himself—whose home is in heaven]. Just as Moses lifted up the [bronze] serpent in the desert [on a pole], so must the Son of Man be lifted up [on the cross], so that whoever believes will in Him have eternal life [after physical death, and will actually live forever] (John 3:13-15 AMP).

"Diane, I admire your spirituality. And I think I believe all the stuff you believe." Karen, a dark haired thirty-something sweet coworker said, as she approached me while I copied papers at the copy machine.

"OK, let's see if you do." I said with a pleasant smile. In my spirit I did not sense she was born again. For some time I had been sharing a little here and there with her from the Bible. But this was our most direct conversation. I was excited to be able to dialogue this openly with her. "Is Jesus the Son of God, Karen?"

"That's what I believe. Oh, I believe everything you believe about Jesus," she said with a big grin.

"Great. Is Jesus God?" I asked.

"Oh, Yes He is!"

"Did He die on a cross? And did He rise from the dead?"

"Yes, I believe that too!"

"Good for you, Karen. These are historical facts a person can believe without any personal accountability. If you don't mind I want to talk about Christ on a more personal level, is that OK?" I asked with a focused gaze into her eyes. She nodded her head.

"Now I want to know if He died on the cross and rose from the dead to make you personally a daughter of God."

"Oh, yeah, of course, we are all daughters or sons of God."

"Yes, we are His children by creation. God is our creator. But we are not all born of Him and have accepted His offer to become born again by asking the Spirit of Christ to come live in us. That is a specific request we must individually make verbally. This is what the Bible says, Karen. Do you believe the Bible was written by people inspired by God?" I asked as I stapled the copies I had made.

"I sure do. See, I told you we believe the same." She remarked as she tapped me on my shoulder.

"Let me ask you the next thing. You said you believe Christ was raised from the dead, and you believe the Bible. Well, the Bible says in Ephesians 1:20, Colossians 3:1, 1 Peter 3:22 and other passages that Jesus Christ is seated at the right-hand of God His Father in heaven, because He is our mediator between us and the judgment of God. Do you understand why He is there as our Mediator to remove God's judgment from us?"

"Well, there's where we disagree. No one knows for sure where Jesus is now."

"Oh? Where do you think He is now? What is He doing after He rose from the dead?"

"I'm not sure He could be living on Pluto."

Trying not to look shocked I asked, "What do you think He is doing on Pluto if He is there?"

"Well, all of us are sons of God. All of us will die and then we're going to rise from the dead. Then we're going to each float to different planets. We will then be in charge of a planet, so I don't know which one Jesus is in charge of right now."

"Karen, I have not found that in the Bible. That kind of puts each one of us on the same level as Christ. He cannot be God if He is no different from any one of us. That is an interesting view. How did you come to that conclusion?"

"Oh, I read a couple of books including the Bible, and took the parts I liked from each book and came to my own conclusion. I believe God allows you to accept what's comfortable for you. I'm happy with my beliefs."

"Oh, I see how with that philosophy *you* might be happy. You still should consider the fact that God wants you to know the truth not simply guess at what *might* be true. The Bible is clear about where Jesus is today and what He came to do for you. You can know for certain if you die tonight whether or not you would go to heaven which is the planet where God lives.

"For salvation that comes from trusting Christ... is as near as our own hearts and mouths. For if you tell others with your own mouth that Jesus Christ is your Lord and believe in your own heart that God has raised him from the dead, you will be saved" (Romans 10:8-10 TLB).

I can share more with you on this subject after work today or anytime if you want."

Karen answered, "No thanks. Anyways my break time is past. I always enjoy talking to you, Diane."

I contemplated as I walked back to my office, *How sad it is to read book after book about Jesus and not take time to see what He actually said about Himself in The Book. Then believe what He said and let that settle your heart. We want things to be complicated when God made it simple. It was hard on Jesus but simple for us.*

It's deadly to presume Jesus is not fully God and fully man. To presume His blood is not eternal and to take anything away from His deity is dangerous. He either is everything the Bible says about Him or it's all a lie. You cannot pick and choose the part you like because then you don't have truth. You have someone other than who He said He is. Yet, that is precisely what is done all around the globe daily.

"Then if anyone says to you, 'Look, here is the Christ!' or, 'Look, He is there!' do not believe it. For false Christs and false prophets will rise and show signs and wonders to deceive, if possible, even the elect. But take heed; see, I have told you all things beforehand" (Mark 13:21-22).

It is dangerous today understanding truth because most religions today have a "Jesus." He may be a good teacher, or a prophet who is no different from any other prophet. The Bible is clear; He shed His eternal blood for us to be redeemed (bought back) from our Enemy. He fought the Enemy for us and won!! He only had to do this once. It took! For Him to need to come and die all over again for us the saints in the last days takes away from His deity and authority with which He conquered death, hell, and the grave. This would mean His blood to cleanse us from sin and the wrath of God was only temporary. Only good until He could come and whip Satan again. One religion says He is the highest form of an arc angel. This belief would mean He was created and had a beginning like all angels.

When the Bible talks about Him in terms of a starting time in the life of Christ it is referring to His humanity—when His eternal Spirit took upon

Himself flesh inside Mary's womb on a certain day and time. The Word of God says He is God and has always existed.

In the beginning [before all time] was the Word (Christ), and the Word was with God, and the Word was God Himself. He was [continually existing] in the beginning [co-eternally] with God. All things were made and came into existence through Him; and without Him not even one thing was made that has come into being (John 1:1-3 AMP).

He had no beginning and will have no end. He is God eternal. In the Book of Revelation He describes Himself as the Alpha and Omega, the beginning and the end.

The Word became flesh and took up residence among us. That's what the word Emanuel means, "God is with us."

We observed His glory, the glory as the One and Only Son from the Father, full of grace and truth (John 1:14 HCSB).

Over the next year Karen came frequently to our weekly lunchtime prayer meeting held by a coworker Sheri and me. She saw undeniable miracles happen for our company and coworkers. I always prayed those seeds would one day take root in her life.

I must tell you what happened as I worked on the last corrections for this chapter. Only God could confirm how much He wants this book in the hands of precious ones like you. I received a call on my business phone from a Texas phone number. My relatives have the same area code so I presumed it was one of them. It was my coworker from the advertisement paper where I worked with Karen! I told her I was thinking about how we both tried to help Karen know how much God loved her. Sheri mentioned the prayer meeting we started and reminded me of some of the miraculous results. I told her I had just written about that.

Joyce was here and I asked her to pick a chapter to read and tell me what she thought. She had chosen this chapter to read because the term deadliest fascinated her. So I had and eye witness of what happened. Here's the clincher Sheri and I have not seen or talked to each other since she moved away in the early 80's. I was so excited my heart was racing. Over the years she looked for me on Facebook and other social media, but I had returned to my maiden name. One day last year she found a picture of me online with the name Gardner. She knew it was me so she googled Diane Gardner and saw I had written a book, *Overcoming the Enemy's Storms.* She purchased it online. She knew my children and former husband and was in awe of what God accomplished through me. She was mesmerized at the level of assaults of the Enemy.

Sheri of Global Dove Ministries said, "God put urgency on my heart to contact you now to tell you what your book meant to me and pray for you."

"She prayed a prayer over this book for a special anointing and decreed its global success. She prayed for me and left me in "happy" tears. Only God could do something like that. Our heavenly Father's timing, love and confirmation to let you know you're doing what He wants leaves me speechless, except to say, WOW! Thank You, Father!

One morning a couple of years ago I met a lovely lady in a coffee house who had a deadly presumption. She was on her way to Yoga class, her name was Valerie. We complimented on each other's gym clothes and struck up a lively conversation. I purchased her iced coffee, and she was so impressed she asked if we could talk a few minutes.

She said, "I can tell you are a deeply spiritual person, so am I, and I'm on my spiritual searching journey."

"Tell me what that means to you," I asked, curious to hear her response. She was intensely involved with Yoga, which has its meditation roots in Buddhism. She also was on a spiritual quest in search of personal spiritual fulfillment and enlightenment. I listened to her speak about her education and her love for "truth," "peace," and "god." She said in a couple of months she was leaving for India in search of many spiritual answers.

We decided to meet together a couple of times before she left. We also became Facebook friends. She said she would post regularly about her "spiritual journey." I wanted to keep in touch.

Before she left the coffee house I told her, "You've mentioned a few questions you are looking for answers to in India. I want to go to India one day. It looks fascinating and I've had friends who were born there and they are all beautiful, even the men." We both laughed.

"Speaking of answers to your questions, I want to know if you currently have your own Bible?

"Yes, I have the one my mom gave me when I was a teenager. It's packed away in one of my boxes in storage." She explained.

"Some of the answers to your spiritual questions are found in your own Bible. It would be good to revisit who Jesus is and why He came." For fifteen minutes I worked to show her what she was looking for was right in her own Bible and not half-way around the world.

She responded, "Oh, of course I know all the things you're sharing with me. I learned all about Jesus when I went to church with my mom as a teenager. I loved hearing it again and I'll add those thoughts to my 'spiritual energy.'"

She thought she knew all about Jesus. I pondered what she told me and thought to myself, *One day I expect to go to India, but not in search of spiritual "enlightenment." She's going where they believe in millions of gods when there is One God who knows and loves her.*

I gave her a booklet on how to become born again. She was adamant there was some mystical answer to life that she could find far away. The claims of Jesus Christ were too simple and took too much humility for it to be all that is required for salvation and righteousness with God. She felt there had to be something to "work" for salvation.

Valerie posted beautiful pictures and her thoughts on her Facebook page for months. She posted several times about one of her early experiences in India when she went to a Hindu temple. She called me when she returned from India. We met at our favorite organic deli.

Valerie shared, "As I sat in the back of the sanctuary of this Hindu temple a terrible eerie feeling came over me. I felt like this blanket came over me and I became frightened. I did what I used to do as a kid when I got fearful—I rocked back and forth. I became increasingly anxious. I decided I had to do something, so to calm my fears I quoted the Lord's Prayer loud enough to hear it with my own ears.

"Suddenly a strong peace came over me. I kept saying the Lord's Prayer until all anxiety was gone. When they were finished I left. I thought the whole thing was really strange."

Valerie excitedly said, "Diane, I wanted to thank you for sending me encouraging notes in response to some of my posts. I really liked them.

"I wanted to make sure you saw one of my early Facebook posts. You know the one about when I was in the Hindu Temple, and I was trembling and could not get any peace until I quoted the Lord's Prayer out loud several times! I'm so glad my mom made me memorize it when I was teenager. I really wanted to get your take on what happened to me when I quoted the Lord's Prayer. Why do you think that brought peace to me?"

I thought, *Finally a great open door. This was her opportunity to understand the power of a biblical passage. She'll know how important it is to memorize the Word like her mom showed her when she was teenager.*

I explained, "The first thing you felt was oppression, which was the eerie feeling that was like a blanket and frightened you. The Bible says in Acts 10:38: *How God anointed Jesus of Nazareth with the Holy Spirit and with power, who went about doing good and healing all who were oppressed by the devil, for God was with Him.*

"The Bible says oppression comes from the devil and Jesus heals us of the oppression. I'm proud of you for recognizing that eerie feeling was *not* from God and *not* for you. Through the words of Jesus came the power that brought you peace.

"He's the one who taught us to address our heavenly Father through that prayer. It is our prayer taught to us by Jesus so it is called, "The Lord's Prayer." The life in those words brought you peace because Jesus is known as the Prince of Peace. The Lord's Prayer brought you closer to the Prince of Peace. You were on your spiritual journey all the way in a foreign country and you found out the greatest spiritual power was still found in the pages of your Bible."

I looked deep into her eyes to see if it looked like she comprehended this powerful truth.

She responded, "Yeah, I have to admit I felt on the inside of me that the Bible was going to make a difference right then, and it did." She put her hand on top of mine.

"You know what? I remember having peace all the rest of that day. Imagine that?" She looked past me while she starred off in a contemplative focus.

"Valerie, within the pages of the Bible is the power, light and life you're looking for. Search the Scriptures. God will send people to help you understand them. He wants you to know the truth."

"Thanks, Diane. I really wanted to understand that incident better and I knew you would know what to tell me."

Shortly after our conversation Valerie and her mom moved away. She abandoned her Facebook page, and we lost all contact. Although she felt God's peace as a tangible thing in her life, she continued her "spiritual journey search." The simple Gospel wasn't enough. I never really got through to her before we lost contact.

I pray for Valerie whenever something reminds me of her. I believe someone else will water the seeds I planted and God will give the increase and, eventually, I believe God will have a harvest.

There are so many people like Karen and Valerie, who hold onto the deadliest presumption—to think that when you die and it is time to answer to God you can give Him your sincere spiritual searching as your basis for eternal life and getting into heaven. It is deadly to be caught dead without Christ.

I watch with curiosity interviews with the "man on the street" by ministries such as Patricia King's XPmedia, Kirk Cameron, Todd White, Chad Daniels, and others. Most people say they believe they know who Jesus is, but are not clear about how He is relevant to their daily lives. If Jesus is not relevant to your daily life then you don't truly know Him. They're not certain if He was born of a virgin. But without the virgin birth he is only a man and His blood would not be eternal.

Everything the Bible says about Jesus we must believe and accept solely by faith. God requires faith. The world says, "Show me, and I will believe." But the world's principles are the opposite of God's principles. Jesus said to Thomas, "Blessed are those who have not seen and yet have believed." We must believe first, and then He shows us the truth.

The first part of my "spiritual journey" was rocky. In my chapter called *My Search* from my book, *Overcoming the Enemy's Storms*. I spewed out my frustrations at God.

"Life is miserable! I heard You're the One who causes everything. If You're the cause of these sicknesses and problems—*leave us alone*. If everything that happens is exactly what *You want* to happen, then You're doing a lousy job of taking care of Your children! My husband almost died at work and experienced first and second degree burns over most of his body. My son has severe asthma attacks and was hospitalized last year for it. I have chronic kidney and bladder infections. My mom is dying of cancer. My brother is killing himself with drugs. I think we would be better off without You! Why would you treat us this way when we are supposed to be Your creation? I would treat my kids better than You treat Yours."

I presumed for years what I heard from others about God was the truth from the Bible. I never took time to look up a single Scripture to see if they were accurate.

I suffered from the deadliest presumption by thinking I was born-again. I presumed because I was a church member, worked in the church, and had been baptized that was sufficient. But I had never confessed with my mouth Jesus as my personal savior.

Even with my stinky attitude I was giving Him my faith by admitting what I believed may not be true and I wanted Him to show me what truth was. I didn't know it but I was emptying myself of my wrong thinking and making room to hear God.

My heart had become calloused. Unresolved presumption leads to bitterness. I had become bitter at life and was becoming bitter at God. I finally opened my heart for the grace of God to come in.

I needed to have some answers: why I needed a Savior and what Jesus came to accomplish. What was I going to do about this information once I received it?

Here are 5 deadly presumptions I overcame to change my life. These are followed by Scripture references that helped me do that.

Presumption 1. I was born-again because I was a church member, worked in the church, and was baptized.

Truth 1. *But what does it say? "The word is near you, in your mouth and in your heart" (that is, the word of faith which we preach): that if you confess with your mouth the Lord Jesus and believe in your heart that God has raised Him from the dead, you will be saved. For with the heart one believes unto righteousness, and with the mouth confession is made unto salvation* (Romans 10:8-10).

None of these verses mentioned salvation or heaven came by church membership, baptism, singing in the choir, or any of my good works. With all my good intentions I still needed to confess with my *own mouth* that Jesus Christ is my savior. And confess that Jesus died for me; shed His precious blood for me, and He rose from the dead for me.

For by grace you have been saved through faith, and that not of yourselves; it is the gift of God, not of works, lest anyone should boast (Ephesians 2:8-9).

I went forward at an altar call at my church. I followed my pastor's wife in this confession, fully trusting I was doing this because she said it was necessary, even though I believed I was already saved. To my surprise within a week I knew something had changed in my relationship with God. I had the Holy Spirit living in me now so I understood spiritual things and the Bible better.

Presumption 2. God was punishing me for the sins for which I had neglected to ask forgiveness. He is mad at me for the sins I committed on purpose.

Self-condemnation and self-pity kept me thinking God was going to permanently withdraw from me.

Truth 2. *"This is how much God loved the world: He gave his Son, his one and only Son. And this is why: so that no one need be destroyed; by believing in him, anyone can have a whole and lasting life. God didn't go to all the trouble of sending his Son merely to point an accusing finger, telling the world how bad it was. He came to help, to put the world right again. Anyone who trusts in him is acquitted; anyone who refuses to trust him has long since been under the death sentence without knowing it"* (John 3:15-18 MSG).

Nothing can separate me from His love. God doesn't have love; He is love. He can be disappointed with me and want me to take a different path. But He always has grace and mercy for me.

Yet in all these things we are more than conquerors through Him who loved us. For I am persuaded that neither death nor life, nor angels nor principalities nor powers, nor things present nor things to come nor height nor depth, nor any other created thing, shall be able to separate us from the love of God which is in Christ Jesus our Lord (Romans 8:37-39).

Presumption 3. The Bible is too hard to learn, and I have a terrible memory, so I can't memorize it anyway.

Truth 3. My mind was undisciplined, and untrained. Therefore I didn't do well holding information and especially the Bible because I have an Enemy who doesn't want me to learn the Word.

But the Helper, the Holy Spirit, whom the Father will send in My name, He will teach you all things, and bring to your remembrance all things that I said to you (John 14:26).

I decided if I could learn commercials and other things I could learn the Word. The key is to learn so we can do according to what is written—not just for the sake of memorization.

I stopped saying, "I can't remember" and started saying "I have a sound mind and the Holy Spirit (my Helper) will bring all things to my remembrance." This faith affirmation made a huge difference.

The best way I've found is to SAY IT with the chapter and verse. PRAY IT with chapter and verse. SING IT with chapter and verse exactly as written. Say it, pray it, and sing it. Do this with the complete passage (thought) if the thought extends beyond one verse. Take several times a day for a few days and it will be sealed into your heart. Then trust the Holy Spirit to bring it to your remembrance when needed. Don't get anxious about remembering the verse you need and say, "Just a moment and the verse will come to me." Allow the Holy Spirit to do His job.

This Book of the Law shall not depart from your mouth, but you shall meditate in it day and night, that you may observe to do according to all that is written in it. For then you will make your way prosperous, and then you will have good success. Have I not commanded you? Be strong and of good courage; do not be afraid, nor be dismayed, for the Lord your God is with you wherever you go" (Joshua 1:8-10).

Presumption 4. The devil will leave me alone if I leave him alone.

Truth 4. The devil hates God and hates us because we are in the image of God. His kingdom of darkness does not leave anyone alone. That is a thought of deception planted by the devil so I wouldn't take my rightful authority over his works. His assaults are calculated. Jesus said:

Take therefore no thought for the morrow: for the morrow shall take thought for the things of itself. Sufficient unto the day is the evil thereof (Matthew 6:34).

Jesus mentioned the Enemy and his works often. He never ignored or took for granted Satan. The Lord knew He could conquer whatever the Enemy tempted Him with by quoting the Scriptures and so can we.

Be sober [well balanced and self-disciplined], be alert and cautious at all times. That enemy of yours, the devil, prowls around like a roaring lion [fiercely hungry], seeking someone to devour (1 Peter 5:8 AMP).

Presumption 5. I'm too young to give up having fun in order to be serious about God. I'll serve God when I get older and it won't matter that I'm bored.

Truth 5. The decisions made when young bring destruction or blessings for the future. When I'm young is the time I make the more important decisions in my life: marriage, career, and children, to trust God or reject Him, keep my virginity or give it away, give in to abusive relationships or love myself and walk away. Those decisions are my foundation and will put my life on course with God or not. Somehow we presume we are invincible when we are young.

I spoke to you in your prosperity, But you said, 'I will not hear.' This has been your manner from your youth, That you did not obey My voice (Jeremiah 22:21).

We develop habit patterns in our youth that help or hinder our relationship with God.

We must stop presuming our decisions as a teenager or young adult are not that serious. STDs are contacted many times as a teen. Other young persons are in prison for a drunken driving accident that ended someone's life or crippled someone. Some have died from being at the wrong place with the wrong person; experimenting with drugs or alcohol can have a lifetime of bad consequences.

Surely, after my turning, I repented; And after I was instructed, I struck myself on the thigh; I was ashamed, yes, even humiliated, Because I bore the reproach of my youth (Jeremiah 31:19).

The principle of reaping what you've sowed was instituted by God from the Garden of Eden. Sow a seed, you will reap a harvest—good or bad, the choice is yours.

Do not be deceived, God is not mocked; for whatever a man sows, that he will also reap. For he who sows to his flesh will of the flesh reap corruption, but he who sows to the Spirit will of the Spirit reap everlasting life. And let us not grow weary while doing good, for in due season we shall reap if we do not lose heart (Galatians 6:7-9).

Pray audibly where you can hear. You will have the confidence you are born again.

Dear heavenly Father, I come to You in Jesus name. I believe Jesus died on the cross and raised from the dead for me, and He is in heaven seated next to You. Lord, Jesus take Your precious blood and cleanse me. Forgive me and heal me. Fill me with Your Holy Spirit. You gave Your life for me now I give my life to You. I will read Your Word, pray for myself and others, and find a Bible based church home. Thank You for loving me.

Tell someone you accepted Christ as your savior. Read your Bible and study some of the passages in this book. Write the date and start writing to your heavenly Father your thoughts, feelings and prayers in a journal.

Is God Really in Control?

Chapter Seven

And we know that all things work together for good to those who love God, to those who are the called according to His purpose (Romans 8:28).

No, God is *not* in control of your responsibilities. Yes, God *is* in control of His responsibilities.

I had a vision while worshiping at home in my early days as a Christian. It opened my understanding about my part in God's economy. I was perplexed about God's sovereignty, my free will, and how they intersect. If God is *entirely* in control and He is sovereign, then when does He want me to do something, and when does He not want me to do anything?

Many Christian clichés about this subject confused me. When am I to "rule with Christ" and go on the offensive to make things happen in the spirit realm? When am I to "be still and know God is in control?" I became worried I was getting in God's way, and on the other hand, anxious I was not doing all He wanted me to do. If you've ever wanted God's will in your life, you've probably experienced some of these anxieties. My vision helped me, and I believe it will help you.

My Vision in Heaven

To help me stay focused and not let my mind wander during my worship time, I painted a picture in my mind of Jesus and me in heaven. In my picture I imagined a huge platform with about 10 steps leading to the stage. Jesus was sitting on a beautiful golden throne facing me and to the right hand of His Father. There was a colorful cloud covering the Father's throne.

And in the midst of the seven lampstands One like the Son of Man, clothed with a garment down to the feet and girded about the chest with a golden band (Revelation 1:13).

I put Jesus in a white robe with a large golden sash around His middle. I wanted Him to look like the description of Him in the Book of the Revelation.

And raised us up together, and made us sit together in the heavenly places in Christ Jesus (Ephesians 2:6).

I tried to be as scriptural as possible when I imagined myself. So I had a throne also, and it was on the crystal clear floor facing their thrones. Mine was a throne exactly like His but much smaller. I was dressed just like Jesus with my white robe and golden sash. I thought to myself, *I need to look like Him because we are joint heirs.*

For you did not receive the spirit of bondage again to fear, but you received the Spirit of adoption by whom we cry out, "Abba, Father." The Spirit Himself bears witness with our spirit that we are children of God and if children, then heirs—heirs of God and joint heirs with Christ, if indeed we suffer with Him, that we may also be glorified together (Romans 8:15-17).

Suddenly the Holy Spirit took over the vision I created and made it into a spiritual revelation that forever changed my views. In the Holy Spirit inspired vision, Jesus rose from His throne and walked down the steps to my throne. I stood to greet Him properly as a King but had no clue of His intentions. He said nothing, but with a pleasant expression on His face reached out His right hand, and I took it with my left hand. He led me up the steps to His throne. He turned around in front of the throne to face forward, so I did the same. He stood in front of His throne, but there was no seat behind me. He looked at me and nodded once. Then He slowly bent over to take His seat. Even though there was no seat for me, I knew He wanted me to do what He did.

I slowly bent over as if to take a seat, and His throne stretched into a "Love Seat" with just enough room for the two of us. I sat on His throne *with* Him— between Him and our Father.

He put His arm around my shoulders like a lover does. He whispered in my ear. "You are a joint heir, an heir of my Father and an equal joint heir of everything given to Me *by* My Father. The picture you painted was wrong. It had you a sub-heir, and My Word does not say you are a sub-heir. We are co-laborers ruling and reigning together."

For we are labourers together with God (1 Corinthians 3:9a KJV).

He turned forward and pointed to the little throne on the floor. He said, "You cannot see what I see from down there. Then He pointed to the vast expanse in front of us and said, "Look and see what I see."

I turned to look out into the heavens, and the earth appeared. Then it zoomed into a country, a city, a house, a family, and then an individual. Everything was in chaos starting with the individual and the individual's chaos spread to take in the surroundings. My heart broke at what I saw, and I was overwhelmed with pain and grief. I knew I was feeling what He felt.

With sadness in His eyes and sternness in His voice He said, "This is *not* My will. I have overcome the world and the Enemy. I have given you the authority to take over for Me as an adopted daughter of God. There are a few things My Father will have the Holy Spirit do from His sovereignty. You have nothing to do with that. But most things are accomplished by you in my stead."

In the next scene, I had my arm around His shoulders and His mine. We had our heads together, planning our warfare strategy about the activities on the earth including my family. I pointed at something and then whispered in His ear my concern. He whispered back His answer. We dealt with one concern at a time. When He spoke I could feel the Holy Spirit getting energized on the inside of me to help me follow through on my instructions. Whatever I heard Him say, I spoke boldly out into the atmosphere.

I spoke, and afterwards I heard the Holy Spirit commission the appropriate angels. I saw their hands shape my God-inspired words into a ball and shove them into the person, the place, or the situation for the will of God to be done. We kept that up until we saw a change in that person, place, or thing.

Then it was His turn. He pointed and showed me His concern. When I understood what was on His heart, He whispered what He wanted spoken in the atmosphere. He also shared whom He wanted me to talk to and what to say. I spoke the words with faith and boldness, and when I did my job my Helper, the Holy Spirit, always did His job. When I did not speak or follow through, my Helper could not respond to the Will of God. The Holy Spirit worked *through* me to accomplish the Will of the Father, not independent of me. Jesus never spoke independent of me either. He had given me His authority on the earth. The vision ended.

We truly were joint heirs. I had much more responsibility than I ever imagined. Then another Scripture came to my understanding.

And Jesus came and spoke to them, saying, "All authority has been given to Me in heaven and on earth. Go therefore and make disciples of all the nations, baptizing them in the name of the Father and of the Son and of the Holy Spirit, teaching them to observe all things that I have commanded you; and lo, I am with you always, even to the end of the age." Amen (Matthew 28:18-20).

Have you ever heard the phrase "God is sovereign?" Well He most definitely is. Sovereign means supreme power and authority. Notice the word *reign* is a part of the word *sovereign.* Reign means to rule and hold royal office. Another word that ties in here is the term "almighty." The word *might* means great and impressive power, strength, or capability. If someone has all the "might" they need for anything at any time, then we can say they are almighty. Even though Hollywood has adopted the term "almighty" for a couple of their movies, God is the only one who totally exemplifies the term. He's got the power!

This reminds me of the story of the man who believed in God's sovereignty to an extreme. One day he was walking down the street and slipped and fell as he stepped up on the curb. He slightly bruised his knee. He got up, brushed himself off, looked up at heaven and said, "Thanks Lord, now we've got *that* part of Your plan for me today out of the way."

I was a recent guest on a television program, and my interviewer was author and speaker, Pam Christian. She made a powerful statement about the sovereignty of God and how easy it is for us to blame Him for everything. Her statement resonated with me, and I asked if I could quote her. Take a moment and meditate on what she said and let it impact you.

Pam said, "Just because God is sovereign over all, doesn't mean He's responsible for all."

God is sovereign, but using the term in a broad sweep that sounds inclusive of everything that happens minimizes the power of Satan—the source of evil. Jesus never ignored His enemy or his ability to wreak havoc. It seems much easier for us to concentrate on God's part and what we "think surely" He ought to do. If we're not careful some can almost think of God like one of the Greek mythological gods that act like humans. When God's sovereignty is so broad, our free will is absent, repentance is unnecessary, and the fact that the world is in its fallen state since it was handed over to the Enemy by Adam and Eve is ignored.

God has self-imposed parameters so He does not violate our free will. If He were going to override anyone's free will by His sovereignty, then He would have slapped the fruit out of Eve's hand and pushed Adam away from temptation. He would have saved Himself a lot of heartache. And ultimately His Son would not have had to die. God having foreknowledge means He knew in advance what would happen, yet, it does not mean what happened is His Will. But you say God allowed it.

We treat this phrase with the same sweeping content we do His sovereignty.

My oldest son, Curtis, a church-going father of two small children is in prison and has been for twenty years, for some serious crimes. I was warned by God the Enemy was planting evil thoughts in my son's mind. I didn't know what the thoughts were, but I knew they were going to be detrimental for his family. I warned him several times. I talked to his pastor, shared my concerns, and asked him to engage Curtis in dialogue to see what he was thinking. He told me to tell Curtis to come see him. Curtis said he would, but didn't. He followed through on those evil thoughts of his own free will. Like Cain, God, true to His nature, warned him that sin was lying at the door of his free will. Curtis heard God's warnings through me and others to stop listening to the Enemy and get counseling for the pain in his heart.

God and I had to "allow" Curtis to do what he chose. Death and life are set before us every day, and the Bible says choose life. Curtis did not do that. He shot his former wife's boyfriend, kidnapped her, and abandoned his children.

God spoke clearly to Cain *before* He killed his brother Abel, but God did not stand between Cain and Able. God is sovereign enough to speak to everyone (saved and unsaved) *every time* they are tempted. I'm sure you remember times you were given a warning before you made a wrong decision. He did this for you even before you were saved. He loves every one of us. His way is to warn us, and our responsibility is to heed the warning. How loving of our heavenly Father to intervene like He does to make that way of escape. But He will not override the gift of free will He has given us. God's interaction with Cain shows exactly how He operates with a violator in any situation. He is God. He never changes. We see here the "law of first mention," which means how a principle is mentioned by God the first time. It usually shows us a pattern that is consistent with His nature.

So the Lord said to Cain, "Why are you angry? And why has your countenance fallen? If you do well, will you not be accepted? And if you do not do well, sin lies at the door. And its desire is for you, but you should rule over it" (Genesis 4:6-7).

Joyce Meyer

Recently on her television program, Joyce Meyer shared a teaching called "Is God Mad at Me?" She shared about God's sovereignty and our free will. I loved some of her comments that apply here.

"We don't hear much teaching about the *will* of a person. We hear a lot about the grace of God. I teach all the time on the grace of God. We cannot do things that please God without His grace. If God asks me to do anything, I can do it with His grace. So I've given up all my dumb excuses for not doing what He says.

"Really, anything we do is because we decided we wanted to. It's all about our free will.

"One of the greatest honors that God has given us is a *free will*. Having a free will is an unbelievably awesome responsibility. Our free-will choices affect us, our children, and our grandchildren."

"Deuteronomy 30:19-20 shows us what to do with our free will—make a choice—choose life.

"I call heaven and earth as witnesses today against you, that I have set before you life and death, blessing and cursing; therefore choose life, that both you and your descendants may live; that you may love the Lord your God, that you may obey His voice, and that you may cling to Him, for He is your life and the length of your days; and that you may dwell in the land which the Lord swore to your fathers, to Abraham, Isaac, and Jacob, to give them."

I wholeheartedly agree with Joyce. Last year my son and his family were some of the stars in their church's Christmas play. They sent me the DVD of the performance. My eyes welled up with tears as I thought that this was made possible because his and his wife's parents chose to bring them up in the

Lord and in church. So the next generation could reap the benefits.

It is important to know that you are a spirit. You have a soul (which is your mind, will, and emotions). And you live in a body. First Thessalonians 5:23 says: *Now may the God of peace Himself sanctify you completely; and may your whole spirit, soul, and body be preserved blameless at the coming of our Lord Jesus Christ.*

Between your mind, will, and emotions, your will is the strongest part of you. Cain's will overrode God's influence, his love for his brother, and his spirit that always wants to obey God.

When we hand out a pound of advice about God's sovereignty, there is usually an ounce of truth in it. So we can feel self-righteous in our advice. However, we presume on God's intention, His motives, and desires. If we were discussing with our friend the death of a brother killed by the other brother we might share one of those Christian clichés to help them feel better. Such as: it was his time to go; God is in control; if he was supposed to live then he would still be alive because God is sovereign, etc. We freely share with others our opinion as if we recently had a discussion with God about His intentions on the matter. We do God an injustice, by our presuming on Him. We can see this was not God's Will because of the conversation He had with Cain. God was Father to both men and His heart was broken when Cain listened to the Enemy and not to Him. Cain put himself under the wrath of God. His way out was the blood of an animal to atone for his sins. Instead he made an offering that had no blood.

Cain did not ask for forgiveness. But I do see where he asked for mercy. God will meet you on the level of your faith. His faith asked for mercy. Though he was a murderer, and under God's judgment, Cain received what He asked for.

And Cain said to the Lord, "My punishment is greater than I can bear! Surely You have driven me out this day from the face of the ground; I shall be hidden from Your face; I shall be a fugitive and a vagabond on the earth, and it will happen that anyone who finds me will kill me."

And the Lord said to him, "Therefore, whoever kills Cain, vengeance shall be taken on him sevenfold." And the Lord set a mark on Cain, lest anyone finding him should kill him (Genesis 4:13-15).

Before I became a Christian I believed some of the statements about God's intent in tragedies and difficult situations. I didn't like the God I heard these statements about. He didn't seem to have love for His own creation. I felt He was playing tricks on us. The following are false statements I've heard all my life—statements quoted in order to bring peace in the midst of turmoil. At times they were spoken as an attempt to provide answers to life's most difficult, unanswered questions. Take a close look. Notice each false statement is a reference to God's sovereignty and releases a person of any responsibility for their actions:

Ounce of Truth 1: "It will all work out for good in the end. Don't worry. God is in control."

God doesn't run behind us or the devil to put out every little fire. Although Romans 8:28 says all things work together for good, this benefit is for those who *love God* and have *chosen* to pursue *His purpose*. The Lord requires faith for Him to act on our behalf and to dispatch angels to intervene. You'll notice most of the healings that Jesus performed in the Gospels are a result of a request of faith. The Lord said in several instances, "Your faith has made you whole." Good does not come from every situation for every person. To make this a blanket statement is misleading.

Ounce of Truth 2: "Things happen for a reason. We don't know what the reason is, but God does."

This is true. God knows the reason everything happens. But it is not true He had a secret reason behind everything that happens. In hindsight so often we see where God warned us by giving us a thought (many call this a gut feeling or your first mind) that we did *not* follow. Afterwards suddenly something goes wrong. The Holy Spirit's job is to help us with everything from little things to saving our lives and the lives of others. Some things were not intended to happen, but they did happen.

Many movies I've seen over the last few years overwork this statement. They make it known they could care less about God, don't seek His wisdom, and violate many of His laws. Then when things go wrong, someone sounds really spiritual. And they say, "I think things happen for a reason, and God will let us know later."

Things do happen for a reason. We may be reaping from the seeds we've sowed—good or bad. The Enemy's plan to steal, kill and destroy. The earth is in a fallen state and unforeseen tragic things can happen. Someone rebelled against what they knew was right. Someone chose evil. Someone chose to be loving and kind.

Ounce of Truth 3: "This happened because God knew He could *trust you* with this tragedy."

This made me want to say I wish He didn't *trust me* so much.

In my book, *Overcoming the Enemy's Storms*, I share several tragic assaults from the Enemy who tried to thwart God's purpose on my life. Some have made this statement to me in an attempt to be complimentary. God chose me to have a calling that would affect many lives so Satan hates that and will always work to keep me from fulfilling my purpose. Since you've chosen to read a book on *Increasing Your Capacity to Hear From God* I am confident that you care about fulfilling God's call on your life and affecting many for Him. Together we have and will continue to destroy the Enemy's assignments over people's lives. God did not have Jesus die so He could turn around and torture us. Jesus was our substitute in order to make us overcomers.

Ounce of Truth 4: "God *took* them because He needed them in heaven." "This was God's appointed time for them to die."

He then would have had to suffer often since the foundation of the world; but now, once at the end of the ages, He has appeared to put away sin by the sacrifice of Himself. And as it is appointed for men to die once, but after this the judgment, so Christ was offered once to bear the sins of many (Hebrews 9:26-28).

This ounce of truth was taken from this passage referring to Jesus dying *once* for our salvation and as a human. The passage also says we only die once. The emphasis is on "once" not on the word *appointed*. We can mistake this to mean your date of death is set, and nothing you do can extend or cut short your life. Many passages give us conditions to be met so we can live longer.

Proverbs 3:1-3 says: *My son, do not forget my law, but let your heart keep my commands; For length of days and long life and peace they will add to you.*

There is no reincarnation, recycling, going to purgatory, or falling into a deep soul sleep. Why would God have Jesus die for us if we got a chance to recycle until we got it right? No, we only get one time to serve our generation and live for God.

I changed my terminology to say: God *received* my love one. Instead of He *took* them.

Ounce of Truth 5: "If something is for you to have (a position, mate, house) it will automatically come to you."

Jesus told us to ask. Our responsibility is to use our faith to ask, seek, and knock. Without our faith we cannot please God, and little to nothing gets done that God wants without our faith. The following is an exciting example of how God requires our words of faith to express our will.

Then many warned him to be quiet; but he cried out all the more, "Son of David, have mercy on me!"

So Jesus stood still and commanded him to be called. Then they called the blind man, saying to him, "Be of good cheer. Rise, He is calling you."

*And throwing aside his garment, he rose and came to Jesus. So Jesus answered and said to him, **"What do you want Me to do for you?"***

The blind man said to Him, "Rabboni, that I may receive my sight."

Then Jesus said to him, "Go your way; your faith has made you well." And immediately he received his sight and followed Jesus on the road (Mark 10:48-52).

Jesus saw the man was obviously blind. Yet He *asked* the blind man what he wanted. Blind Bartimaeus could have said he had a migraine and wanted healing for his headache. He could have asked for prayer for one of his children. Jesus was pleased to meet his need no matter what he wanted, because faith pleases God. Even if Bartimaeus remained blind, but had his request answered and testified of God's goodness, it would have encouraged many to believe God for themselves.

The skeptics will be the same whether his testimony was his sight or something else. God is glorified when we ask in faith. We have a free will, and Jesus demonstrated how He respected blind Bartimaeus' will and did not override it by assuming what he wanted. I think that is excellent.

Ounce of Truth 6: "God only helps the weak. The rest of us should figure things out and only bother God when it is an emergency or too big for us to handle."

God loves us deeply so there are many Scriptures that admonish us to make right choices, learn God's ways, and receive corresponding rewards. Choosing God's ways come with each small decision. Otherwise by the time we call on Him we've made a mess.

Ounce of Truth 7: "Everyone's path is completely directed by God."

Proverbs 3:5-6 says: *Trust in the Lord with all your heart, and lean not on your own understanding; In all your ways acknowledge Him, And He shall direct your paths.*

If the slightest conditions for a god-fearing life have not been met how can we say we are directed by God? This passage admonishes us to acknowledge God, not *inform* Him of *our* plans. We need to acknowledge He is God and surrender to Him before we draw any conclusions of what we will do and what's best.

Now this is the confidence that we have in Him, that if we ask anything according to His will, He hears us (1 John 5:14).

What is the condition to getting our prayers heard and answered? We ask according to His will that is found in His Word.

For it is not your strength, but it is God who is effectively at work in you, both to will and to work [that is, strengthening, energizing, and creating in you the longing and the ability to fulfill your purpose] for His good pleasure (Philippians 2:13 AMP).

He's working in us all the time. Let's work with Him. I love the Amplified Bible on this verse when it says, "creating in you the longing." This means you allow Him to help you change your desires to want what He wants for you.

Prayer: Today I surrender my desires to You. Today I will not harden my heart to go my own way, finding my own pleasure and speaking my own words. I will delight in You and honor You by doing what Your Word says for me to do. I will delight in You today, Lord. Holy Spirit, You are my Helper, and I will let You help me by taking heed to Your nudges and thoughts. I choose to be called according to Your purpose. I love You and will receive the rewards.

The Worst Presumption Ever!

Chapter Eight

Be alert and of sober mind. Your enemy the devil prowls around like a roaring lion looking for someone to devour. Resist him, standing firm in the faith, because you know that the family of believers throughout the world is undergoing the same kind of sufferings (1 Peter 5:8-9 NIV).

"The devil made me do it!" Carlton, my six year old, said to the Christian Education Director when asked why he was sitting in a chair outside his Sunday school classroom.

"The teacher put me out here. But it's not my fault!" He exclaimed while making a fist with his right hand and slamming it into his left. "The devil made me do it! So when I catch him, I'm going to sock him back to hell where he belongs!"

"The devil made me do it!" was a phrase made popular in the early 70s by Geraldine, one of Flip Wilson's characters on The Flip Wilson Show. We laughed hysterically each time Geraldine used the phrase to escape responsibility for her wrongdoing.

Today some people presume the word devil is simply a catchall phrase for evil in the world. It's as though Satan himself ceased to exist in our minds with the advent of the post-modern age. We think we're too educated and too technologically savvy to believe in such an archaic thing as a "real being" called Satan. Some of us think there is no such thing as something supernatural like that. We presume everything can be rationally explained away.

The worst presumption ever is to presume the devil is not a real person with a kingdom, one third of the angels, other disembodied spirits (not ghosts), and that he is not behind influencing all the evil in the world.

Jesus contrasts what He does versus how the Enemy operates in John 10:10 which says: *The thief does not come except to steal, and to kill, and to destroy. I have come that they may have life, and that they may have it more abundantly.*

Some of us do not believe Satan is real and have never taken the time to understand who he is or how he operates. But all of a sudden when tragedy strikes we can be the first to comfort someone with what God's intent is in the situation. In our attempt to make something good out of a bad situation, we presume and put words in God's mouth that He never said. In this way we presume on God big time. Another danger is we presume a statement about who God is and what He desires is true because we saw it on the Internet or heard it from a trusted relative or friend. We think it's true because our pastor said it when we were young, or maybe a sports figure or movie star we admire spoke the presumption. When influential people spoke presumptuously in the Old Testament God instructed the leaders to stone them to death. Ouch! This was serious to God because it contaminated the people and led them astray from the truth.

On the other hand, there are those of us who believe strongly in the supernatural, but still don't believe there is a devil. The assumptions drawn by this thinking are every spiritual force comes from God and He directly orchestrates everything that happens. This is what my mom felt and how she got caught up in the Occult through astrology and fortunetellers. It opened the door to demonic activity in our home. Then we conclude that every supernatural event, and even that every psychic, fortuneteller, medium, astrologer, demonic apparitions, and horoscope predictions are from God. Familiar spirits are familiar with people and can give information and it is not from the Lord.

So the two schools of thought we're focusing on here: First, the devil is only a negative force of the mind of collective negative mental influence in the Universe. Second, all supernatural influences are directly from God whether good or evil. Therefore, there is no being called Satan. These two extremes are the worst presumptions ever!

There is no doubt the Enemy exists if our foundation is the Bible. Jesus and the apostles were specific about the evil one. Various Bible references express this.

So, my dear children don't let anyone divert you from the truth. It's the person who acts right who is right, just as we see it lived out in our righteous Messiah. Those who make a practice of sin are straight from the Devil, the pioneer in the practice of sin. The Son of God entered the scene to abolish the Devil's ways [works] (1 John 3:7-8 MSG).

No amount of meditative chanting, Hindu or Buddhist practice of sitting in asana or lotus positions, following expensive and tedious rituals to become "clear," or speaking to the Universe is going to rid the world of the effects of the Enemy's works. Only the name and blood of Jesus can destroy his works.

Jesus did not come to destroy the devil himself. Satan is a spirit, and spirits cannot die. They exist forever. You are a spirit. You have a soul (which consists of your mind, will, and emotions), and you live in a body. Your body will eventually die. Your spirit and soul will live forever in the presence of your Father. You'll live with your Father God in heaven or your father "god" below.

Where did Satan come from and what is his intent? Without getting too theological, Satan was like Darth Vader he started off on the good side of the Force and went rogue. His name was Lucifer and he was one of three arc angels the highest form. He cannot create anything only pervert what God had created. He took passion and humility and perverted them to jealousy and pride the original sins. Jesus had to take His blood to cleanse the heavenly utensils of worship because Lucifer was in charge of worship in heaven. He still uses jealousy and pride as some of his best tools of destruction. He wants to be worshiped like God is worshiped. He was cast out into the earth and Adam and Ever were supposed to take dominion over him. That's why he hid inside a serpent and used deception because he knew they could kick him out if they knew it was him in Genesis 3.

Revelation 12:9-12 tells us: *So the great dragon was cast out, that serpent of old, called the Devil and Satan, who deceives the whole world; he was cast to the earth, and his angels were cast out with him.*

Then I heard a loud voice saying in heaven, "Now salvation, and strength, and the kingdom of our God, and the power of His Christ have come, for the accuser of our brethren, who accused them before our God day and night, has been cast down. And they overcame him by the blood of the Lamb and by the word of their testimony, and they did not love their lives to the death. Therefore rejoice, O heavens, and you who dwell in them! Woe to the inhabitants of the earth and the sea! For the devil has come down to you, having great wrath, because he knows that he has a short time."

When we deny the existence of a real devil, the only one left to blame for the evil in the world is God. This makes God look schizophrenic—good one day and bad the next.

"War Room" is a movie about no longer ignoring our real Enemy, Satan. The main character, Elizabeth Jordan, is asked by her elderly client Miss

Clara, "How's your prayer life? Would you say it is hot or cold?"

Her response was, "I wouldn't say it is hot or cold... I'm like most people."

To emphasize her point to Elizabeth of the importance of prayer, Miss Clara serves her a lukewarm cup of coffee that makes her gag. She asks, "Miss Clara, do you like your coffee room temperature?"

Miss Clara answers, "No, I don't. Mine is hot."

Miss Clara demonstrates her point about how lukewarm coffee is distasteful to us, so we should consider how much our lukewarm prayer life is distasteful to God.

Every one of us is lukewarm at times. The danger is in choosing to stay complacent and never making the choice to find out what God feels about our approach to life's issues. Our will is the strongest part of us. We can make choices to say and act in ways that overcome our wrong feelings.

Revelation 3:16 is Jesus' response to us when we get lukewarm: *So then, because you are lukewarm, and neither cold nor hot, I will vomit you out of My mouth.*

These are strong words. Jesus makes it painfully clear how He feels when we ignore what His Word says about the authority over our Enemy, which He has purchased for us. When we don't fight, we are choosing to abdicate victory for others and ourselves. Instead, we choose comfort. When we stay lukewarm for an extended period of time, we also become self-righteous and self-deceived. Eventually we can become unteachable know-it-alls. We know just enough to do disservice to the Kingdom of God and turn others away from the Bible.

But be doers of the word, and not hearers only, deceiving yourselves (James 1:22).

A person who is cold doesn't know any better. They don't know the Word and may not have heard about the power in the name of Jesus and in His Word. They are easier to convince about their need for a spiritual awakening than the lukewarm. The name of Jesus may only be used as a swear word to them. I wonder why people don't swear and say, Oh Buddha! Oh Scientology! Or Hinduism! Nope, the goal is to water down the power in His name. Faith in the name of Jesus is the only name that can destroy Satan's works. So guess who chose that precious Name (Jesus) and His title, Christ (the Anointed One), as a common swear word?

A person who is hot is passionate about God's Kingdom purpose on the Earth. These people are using the weapons the Lord gave us to fight the Enemy. But when we become lukewarm we still have the weapons right at our disposal, but we refuse to open our mouths and join the fight. The Enemy can deceive us into thinking we won't make a difference in our problems or in the problems of others.

When we are lukewarm we are usually the first ones to blame God when tragedy strikes. We don't consider that our fight of faith could have averted some or all of the attack of the Enemy.

Now this, "He ascended"—what does it mean but that He also first descended into the lower parts of the earth? He who descended is also the One who ascended far above all the heavens, that He might fill all things (Ephesians 4:9-10).

Why did Jesus descend to the lower parts of the earth and when did He do that? He went there after His death and before His resurrection. He took the authority away from Satan which was represented by "keys." These were not literal keys. But Jesus took back the authority to humanity and the Earth that Adam and Eve turned over to Satan. *Jesus expressed this:*

I am He who lives, and was dead, and behold, I am alive forevermore. Amen. And I have the keys of Hades and of Death (Revelation 1:18).

He conquered for us and now we conquer the forces of evil for Him. To bind their kings with chains, And their nobles with fetters of iron; To execute on them the written judgment—
This honor have all His saints. Praise the Lord! (Psalm 149:8-9).

It's been my experience that the lukewarm persons are the ones who come up with some kind of religious verbiage that is not scriptural, nor is it consistent with God's nature. When a problem arises, we shift all the responsibility onto God and place none on ourselves. A poignant verse we should hold on to is found in 1 Timothy 6:12: *Fight the good fight of faith, lay hold on eternal life, to which you were also called and have confessed the good confession in the presence of many witnesses.*

Instead of taking a stand in spiritual things we make statements like, "I don't know why God let this happen. Or God sent this tragedy because He's trying to teach you something." Or "God works in mysterious ways." Or "Everything happens for a reason, so it will all work out." Or "God needed your loved one so He could have another member in heaven's choir." Or "God knew this child was going to grow up and do wrong so He took him while he was still innocent."

Before I was saved it was statements like these that caused me to build resentment toward God. Was He for me or against me? Was He rewarding me or punishing me? Why tell me God loves me and then try to "comfort" me with statements about how He is destroying me?

People on television, radio, coworkers, relatives, etc. who may not have picked up a Bible in ages suddenly become "experts" at presuming what God is thinking and why things have happened. They have certainly never studied the Word to see what God truly says about Himself. They pray according to their feelings sometimes with repetitious vain prayers to God like He is a vending machine who spits out answers to prayers when we put in the right "coin."

In searching the Scriptures about God's Will, I've discovered God never overrides the will of a person. He gives us choices. Before Cain slew Able, God came to him and reasoned with him to make the right choice. God's conversation with Cain reveals how God warns through words or impressions, and then He leaves the choice up to us.

If you do well, will you not be accepted? And if you do not do well, sin lies at the door. And its desire is for you, but you should rule over it (Genesis 4:7).

This is always the way He has chosen to operate—speak a warning or send someone to speak the warning to us and then leave the choice up to us. If God was ever going to override the will of man in order to aggressively assert His will, He would have slapped the fruit out of Adam and Eve's hands. Canceling the original sin would have saved God a lot of heartache and the death of His Son.

We cannot make God into who we want Him to be. That's how mankind came up with Greek Mythology, making our gods to act like humans. Jesus became flesh, just like us, but remained God. Therefore, although a man, He resisted every temptation of the flesh and was sinless!

When we are lukewarm we presume we are full of faith, but the Holy Spirit knows we're not doing the works that bear fruit and get results. We must add works to our faith.

What does it profit, my brethren, if someone says he has faith but does not have works? Can faith save him?...Thus also faith by itself, if it does not have works, is dead. Show me your faith without your works, and I will show you my faith by my works. You believe that there is one God. You do well. Even the demons believe—and tremble! But do you want to know, O foolish man, that faith without works is dead? (James 2:14-20).

In Our Mind, Memory, and Mouth Is Our Miracle.

Derek Prince

In the book titled, Derek Prince on *Experiencing God's Power*, it says, "Satan has a highly organized kingdom. He has rulers with descending orders of authority and sub-rulers responsible for different areas of their territories. That is a staggering fact, but it is quite clear. The fact that Satan heads a highly organized kingdom astonishes some people."

Take time to read with intent what the Bible says about how to discover the two Kingdoms. The Kingdom of Darkness also referred to as the Kingdom of the Law of Sin and Death versus the Kingdom of Light also referred to as the Kingdom of His Dear Son, Kingdom of God, Kingdom of Heaven, and the Kingdom of the Law of Life in Christ Jesus. These are the only forces that govern our planet and the entire universe.

Jesus gave clear instructions that there is a constant battle, and we must fight whether we want to or not. I was not a fighter growing up. I have never been in a physical fight in my life. I always talked others out of fighting me. Even as an adult I was easily intimidated and hated confrontations.

At the time I was born again my emotional pattern was to allow people and circumstances to run over me. Yet in my Bible reading I kept seeing confrontations. I hated confrontations. Then the Holy Spirit challenged me to understand that Jesus came to make me a warrior and not a wimp. The Bible was obvious; if I wanted to please God, I had to learn to desire to have victory. I needed to determine to live the life of an overcomer. My mind had to become renewed to the Word and not allow my feelings to govern me.

In Joni Lamb's interview with Joyce Meyer, on her television show *Joni's Table Talk,* Joyce said, "You have nothing to change your mind from the lies of the Enemy if you don't take time to know the Word."

Jesus taught, "Assuredly, I say to you, among those born of women there has not risen one greater than John the Baptist; but he who is least in the kingdom of heaven is greater than he. And from the days of John the Baptist until now the kingdom of heaven suffers violence, and the violent take it by force" (Matthew 11:11-12).

Our Mind: Our natural thoughts are the opposite of what God desires. So we must make a decision to renew our minds. Study what the Bible says about who we are in Christ. Study what the Bible says about our real Enemy. Study about our victory over Satan.

For we do not wrestle against flesh and blood, but against principalities, against powers, against the rulers of the darkness of this age, against spiritual hosts of wickedness in the heavenly places (Ephesians 6:12).

Our Memory: I had a horrible memory growing up. My family said I was senile since I was ten-years-old. John 14:26 was my answer: *But the Helper, the Holy Spirit, whom the Father will send in My name, He will teach you all things, and bring to your remembrance all things that I said to you.*

The Holy Spirit helps me remember. Remember the little memorization key I gave you? Quote the Word. Quote exactly as it is written along with the chapter and verse. SAY IT, SING IT, AND PRAY IT. By the time you do this three times a day for three days—you've got it! You might start with some of the Scriptures in this chapter. Remember to stop saying "I forgot, or can't remember." Say it will come back to me in a moment.

Our Mouth: Say out loud what the Bible says about you, about Satan, and about circumstances. Proverbs 18:18-20 says: Death and life are in the power of the tongue. Everything we see was originally created by words. When your words are in alignment with God's Word you can resist the Enemy and he will flee. You create your future with your mouth.

Our Miracles: God has Miracles for you! Be thankful every day the Holy Spirit has a plan of victory for you. Praise Him, and His grace will be activated.

My brethren, count it all joy when you fall into various trials, knowing that the testing of your faith produces patience (James 1:2).

Rejoice always, pray without ceasing, in everything give thanks; for this is the will of God in Christ Jesus for you (I Thessalonians 5:16-18).

This verse says "in" everything give thanks because God has your answer. Not "for" everything because God did not cause evil. Whatever Jesus did in the Gospels is truth. He didn't make anyone sick, nor did He steal, kill, or destroy. He asked for sacrificial lying down of finances, family, and personal desires. This is surrendering and will be rewarded. This is not stealing from us.

Psalm 91 says you tread (walk) on serpents (Satan is referred to as a serpent). Use the power given to us through God's Word. Watch out for presumption because the miracle may not come the way you except. Miracles happen when we use the power given to us in the Name of Jesus, and we release the power of the blood of Jesus through quoting the Scriptures against the Kingdom of Darkness. Declare the Kingdom of God shall prevail!

Presumptions and Traditions

Chapter Nine

Making the word of God of no effect through your tradition which you have handed down. And many such things you do (Mark 7:13).

Remember the musical play *Fiddler on the Roof*? After expressing some of the ways his community handled life and trained their children, the Patriarch of the community turned to the audience and asked, "How do we keep our balance? That, I can tell you in one word—traditions!"

He expressed there were traditions for everything. Yet he admitted, "None of us have a clue how most of our traditions got started."

Somehow if we like or are comfortable with our traditions we presume God is happy because we are. We have to admit that is the way it is in our service for the Lord. We haven't a clue how it got started or if it is rooted in God's Word. It's just what we do and the way we do it. Tradition!

One of my favorite professors in Bible College challenged me continually to expand my capacity to hear from God. He gave us an illustration about tradition I have never forgotten.

Dr. O. Cope Budge said, "Suppose you were a well-known teacher who studied crows for years. You had even written books on the life and habits of black crows. Your professors before you laid the groundwork for your study of black crows. You had done tons of research on black crows and your research papers, books, and lectures all stated that there are only black crows in the world.

"What if one day you were outside and you saw with your own eyes a white crow? What would you do? You make most of your money telling about black crows. You have three possible responses.

"First, you can lie to yourself because of pride and tell yourself that was a different bird and not a crow. Second, you can let go of your previous teachings and traditions and admit to yourself you've seen a white crow but decide to only tell someone when the subject comes up. This is still pride. Or three, you can admit you acted upon the knowledge you had and you have received further knowledge. God created white crows that you didn't know existed. Show from a heart of humility your willingness to let go of your tradition and former teaching. Your future depends on your willingness to be teachable and ability to let go when necessary."

The Bible is full of traditions. Some were instituted by God and require faith, represent Christ, and reveal truths about the Kingdom of God. Others were instituted by men to make them feel religious or in control.

Jesus said to the religious leaders of His day, the Pharisees and scribes, their (man-made) traditions "make the Word of God of no effect." How can something be more powerful than God's Word? That's not possible. How do we know this? What did Jesus say about His Words?

Heaven and earth will pass away, but My words will by no means pass away (Luke 21:33).

So how does tradition cancel the effectiveness of the Word? What actually happens is the power found in the Bible must be actively released by putting a demand on its power through an intentional activation of your faith. There is a great example of this in Acts 3 when Peter and John went to the Temple to pray and a lame man whom they probably had passed for years was there. The Bible says he was laid daily at the gate Beautiful. Peter gave a command to the man that would help the lame man get focused so his heart was open with expectation (hope).

And fixing his eyes on him, with John, Peter said, "Look at us." So he gave them his attention, expecting to receive something from them. Then Peter said, "Silver and gold I do not have, but what I do have I give you: In the name of Jesus Christ of Nazareth, rise up and walk." And he took him by the right hand and lifted him up, and immediately his feet and ankle bones received strength.

So he, leaping up, stood and walked and entered the temple with them—walking, leaping, and praising God... Now as the lame man who was healed held on to Peter and John, all the people ran together to them in the porch which is called Solomon's, greatly amazed...

And His name [Jesus], through faith in His name, has made this man strong, whom you see and know. Yes, the faith which comes through Him has given him this perfect soundness in the presence of you all (Acts 3:4-8; 11; 16).

Peter said it was through faith which comes through Jesus that healed the lame man. Peter took time to put a demand on all the Name of Jesus represents by his intentional activation of faith. He also helped the man open his heart to expectation with hope and faith to receive "something." When Peter told him to look on them he was helping the man prepare for his miracle. If Peter had leaned on the traditional response to the poor and had only given him silver and gold, the man would have died crippled. Today we hear the Name of Jesus spoken as a swear word or a simple comment in a sentence. This has become our tradition. Peter didn't say the Name of Jesus made that man whole. Some people spoke the name of Jesus in hatred in those days. He said *faith in the Name of Jesus* which overcame tradition and released the power in His name.

Here are two extreme presumptions people have shared that can cancel the effectiveness of the Word:

False Presumption 1. "God doesn't need to do miracles anymore because modern medicine is so much more advanced today than in Bible times."

False Presumption 2. "God doesn't need medicine to bring healing to us. He is not pleased with us when we go to the doctor and take medication. That isn't the best kind of faith."

My cousin, who loved the Lord and had just turned fifty-years-old, died recently because she trusted in false presumption #2. She refused medical help for some serious health issues. She had a wonderful church home with great balanced teaching in the Word. But early in her Christian walk she was influenced by some faulty traditions and teaching on healing. Later in life when sickness was an issue she presumed her early teachers were more accurate than her current teachers. She also ignored her family who begged her to believe God by faith *and* take the medication available to her also. We were heartbroken that her wrong traditions based on a wrong presumption cut her life short.

There is a way that seems right to a man, But its end is the way of death (Proverbs 16:25).

When we are stuck in tradition we never go to the core truth or secret counsel of God's love revealed on a level that changes lives. We are like the character in *Fiddler on the Roof* who said to the audience, "Where did these traditions come from?" His answer to us was, "I don't know."

It's good to examine our traditions and give God the opportunity to let us know which ones we need to let go of, so we can replace the tradition with a deep level truth. Why do we do what we've always done? Is it based on His word?

Let's consider a story I've heard told.

The new bride prepared to cook a roast for her husband. Before she put it in the roasting pan she cut two inches off each end and threw them in the trash. She seasoned the rest of the meat and put it in the oven.

Leaning against the kitchen counter watching his wife her new husband was puzzled, "Sweetheart, why would you throw away perfectly good meat?"

She answered, "Because we don't need it."

"Why don't we need it?"

She shrugged her shoulders. "I don't know, I'll ask my mom because she's the one who taught me to cook our roasts this way." She went to the phone and called. "Mom, Daniel wants to know why we cut the ends off our roasts when it is good meat."

Her mom paused. "Ah, I'm not sure, honey. Ask grandma because when I was growing up she's the one who made sure I always cut the ends off."

She called her grandma to eagerly ask the question she had never needed an answer to before. "Grandma, Daniel wants to know why we always cut the ends off of the roast. Mom said she didn't know and you would."

"Well, honey, I didn't know your mother was still carrying on that practice. It looks like she has made it a tradition and passed it on to the next generation. The truth is, when she was growing up the only roasting pan we had was a medium-sized one, and the store didn't carry a larger one. So the roasts never fit into the pan. We cut the ends off so the roasts would fit.

"I figured when your mom got married she'd buy a larger roasting pan and would have no need to cut off the ends.

"I never thought she'd make it into a family *tradition* and you'd call me about it years later." She said with a chuckle in her voice.

I believe the Holy Spirit admonishes us to continually examine our traditions to see if they conflict with the Word of God. Are we willing to stop the presumption our tradition is based on and make room for truth to take its place? This will increase our capacity to make room for faith to grow.

I thank God I don't need to rely on traditions and religious clichés to tell me what God will and won't do. When I realize I'm thinking God will move the way I have presumed, I can let go and have a paradigm shift, which broadens my perception on His Word and His Will.

Letting go of tradition to receive a paradigm shift increases our capacity to believe.

I got excited about a testimony I recently heard at our ASCEND Conference at the Angelus Temple in Los Angeles. It was a personal testimony I had originally heard the speaker's father give in the late 70s. I also read it many times in his books.

The testimony was by Rev. Lisa Osteen Combs, Joel Osteen's sister, and daughter to Pastor John and Dodie Osteen. I asked her if I could use her powerful story in this book and she graciously gave me her permission of how they overcame false pre-sumption #1.

Lisa said the umbilical cord cut off her wind at birth. The doctors diagnosed her as having problems similar to that of Cerebral Palsy. She had no sucking action, couldn't lift her head, and couldn't roll over. As she grew she was not able to sit up. The specialists said she would never walk or talk.

She said, "My parents desperately wanted me to be healed to whatever level of function God would allow. But they thought if God could make me a 'little better' then why not 'all the way better?'"

"The problem was their tradition taught them miracle healing was a thing of the past. They were told the 'Day of Miracles' was no longer needed because of the advent of medical science. The problem was I was beyond what medical science could do. My dad took off his traditional, denominational, religious glasses and instead of reading the Bible through those glasses of tradition he began to say, 'God show me who You really are.'

"He saw healing passages he had never noticed. So Dad and Mom concentrated on the Gospels which show healing Scriptures and Christ healing many people. Dad saw in John 10:10 where Satan is the Enemy. He also saw where Hebrews 8:5 says: *Jesus Christ the same, yesterday, today, and forever.* That set him free right there. Then with Mom and his newfound faith they set the time and the day that they would activate their faith to believe God without any doubt. They prayed for healing for me and believed God that His Word was working on me. They didn't see any immediate changes but they still trusted in faith.

"They repeated to God. 'Jesus, if you healed back then you can heal our daughter today.'

"It didn't happen overnight, but gradually healing happened over the next few months.

"I began to change. I began to move my arms and my legs. I lifted my head, finally. They could see my muscles begin to fight back. By the time I was one year old I was completely normal, completely healed.

"My parents sought the Bible for themselves. For years I went back to the pediatrician and every time she would see me she'd say, 'There's the miracle girl.' Because she knew what a miracle it was."

Lisa Osteen Combs has no residual affect from her childhood crippling disease.

At the conference Lisa concluded with these words of wisdom, "Don't blame God for what Satan does. James 4:7 says, 'Resist him and he will flee' in the Name of Jesus! Sometimes we have to let go of what others have taught us which becomes our tradition if it doesn't line up with the Word of God.

They can only teach us what they know. You can read the Bible for yourself. That's what my parents did, to find out the truth of God's Word, and they pressed pass their *traditions*.

"To share their new found faith my parents left the church they were pastoring and started Lakewood Church for people to experience the truth of the Word and the power of the Holy Spirit for themselves. They wanted people to know there wasn't a 'Day' of miracles that is passed, but know that we serve a 'God' of miracles."

Pastor John Osteen came up with a confession to help us value what the Bible says about us.

This is *my* Bible; I am what it says I am and I can do what it says I can do!

Too Familiar To See

Chapter Ten

All spoke well of Him and were amazed at the gracious words that came from His lips. "Isn't this Joseph's son?" they asked. Jesus said to them, "Surely you will quote this proverb to Me: 'Physician, heal yourself! Truly I tell you," he continued, "no prophet is accepted in his hometown" (Luke 4:22-24NLT).

You've probably heard the life (not biblical) proverb: Familiarity breeds contempt which means extensive knowledge of or close association with someone or something leads to a loss of respect for them or it.

I've discovered a hard lesson to live by and that is: Being too familiar with someone can lead me to presume they are just doing their usual talking and not speaking to me on God's behalf. I know I've missed some messages God was bringing to me by ignoring the vessel He had chosen.

This glared in my face one day as a young Christian. I wanted God to be the prominent one in my life and do things His way. I was at my mom's house when I learned an important lesson.

"Curtis, come here," my mom said as she beckoned for her oldest grandson to come to her bedside. My mother was bedridden because of cancer of the spine, and I was her main caregiver. School was out so I had my two sons, Curtis and Carlton, with me as I cooked, cleaned, and took care of her.

"Are those iron-on patches on the knees of your pants?" she asked as she grabbed his left pant-leg to take a closer look. Before he could answer her she fired another question at him. "Did you wear these pants to school with those patches on them?"

"Yes." Curtis responded to both questions.

"Bring me my purse, Curtis, so I can give your mom some money. I don't want you looking like a motherless child any longer."

I felt the need to defend myself as I stepped closer to the bed so we could see each other eye-to-eye. "Mom, thank you for the offer, but I don't need your money. Besides iron-on patches are a part of the fun look these days. People put them on everything. God will provide money when Curtis needs new pants. These pants are practically new." I mustered up the best little smile I could.

She asked, "Is there a hole in one of the legs of his pants you are covering up with those patches?"

"Ah, yeah."

"Then take this money and buy that boy some decent pants. This should be enough for two pair." Turning to Curtis she said, "Here give this money to your mom. You don't ever need to go to school with torn clothes. You just tell your grandma and I'll help you."

I felt humiliated. I said, "Thank you, but we pray, and God helps us."

I thought, *He doesn't humiliate me while He's blessing me. Next time I'll have more faith and I won't need your money. The Bible says in Proverbs 10:22: The blessing of the Lord makes one rich, and He adds no sorrow with it. God doesn't add sorrow with his gifts.*

On my drive home I kept replaying our conversation in my head and getting angry because my mom seemed to love humiliating me. Then I could feel the Holy Spirit wanted to tell me something. I turned the car radio off and got quiet.

I heard these words: *Does your mom love you? Is she available for Me to use her as My answer to your prayers? Don't resist your blessings through pride. Don't rebel because you don't like the way and through whom it is delivered. Remember I'm using flawed vessels that may obey Me, but do it their way. Watch out for being too familiar with someone and overlooking what I can do through them.*

I repented and stopped presuming on the familiar vessels God was using to answer my prayers, especially my mother. She never changed her ways, but I learned not to presume she would be any different. Her words may have hurt but I released them to the Lord immediately and did not nurse or rehearse them. I renounced their influence and refused to let her ways bother me anymore. This helped us have a better relationship the last couple years of her life.

Jesus faced His family and closest friends as the first people to whom He announced a hidden truth about Himself. They refused to believe God could use Him as the answer to their prayers for the coming Messiah, healer, and king.

He came to fulfill the Law of God. So after defeating the Enemy in the wilderness He went to His hometown synagogue as His custom was, but this time He had a special message. This thirty-year-old rabbi now could legally take a leadership role and reveal what that role was.

The majority of the community could not embrace God using a lowly carpenter's son to be a world changer. Their over familiarity caused them to presume on God in a way that cost them dearly.

Over familiarity can become the basis for us to presume and miss God.

We so easily do the same as those in Nazareth. We tune out our parents, children, friends, coworkers, bosses, or mate when looking for wisdom from the Lord. We may be reminded by the Holy Spirit of something they said in the past when we need guidance. But because we don't realize how the Holy Spirit works, we override the insight given. Often He unlocks *their voice* from our memory, and we hear their words in their voice on the inside of us. Then we think it's just them that we are hearing, and we ignore or reject what we've heard.

Everyone was impressed by how well Jesus spoke. But they were surprised at his presumption to speak as a prophet, so they said among themselves, "Who does he think he is? This is Joseph's son, who grew up here in Nazareth." Jesus said to them, you'll say, "Work the miracles here in your hometown.' But let me tell you, no prophet is welcomed or honored in his own hometown (Luke 4:22-24 TPT).

Jesus was quoting from what they all knew was a prophecy about the Messiah found in Isaiah. To us it is Isaiah 61:1-3. In Luke 4:18-21 Jesus dared to end His time of reading with an unexpected announcement.

"The Spirit of the Lord is upon Me, because He has anointed Me to preach the gospel to the poor; He has sent Me to heal the brokenhearted, to proclaim liberty to the captives and recovery of sight to the blind, to set at liberty those who are oppressed; to proclaim the acceptable year of the Lord." Then He closed the book, and gave it back to the attendant and sat down. And the eyes of all who were in the synagogue were fixed on Him.

And He began to say to them, "Today this Scripture is fulfilled in your hearing."

Luke 4: 28-30 TPT shows how deeply they presumed on Jesus. How can He be the Messiah when He is just a hometown boy? They were too familiar with Him to "see" Him for who He was.

When everyone present heard those words, they erupted with furious rage. They mobbed Jesus and threw him out of the city, dragging him to the edge of the cliff, ready to hurl him off. But he walked right throughout the crowd, leaving them all stunned (Luke 28-30 TPT).

Often we are the victim of someone presuming on us—who we are and what we are about. And then there are the times when we are the one presuming—who someone else is and what they are about, or whether or not God can use them in our lives.

I remembered over thirty years ago a young woman and her family became a member of the church I was attending. Betty was a gifted young mother who was an independent hairdresser. Through the women's ministry at the church we got to know each other.

She became increasingly hungry for God's purpose for her life. Betty started to pray prayers of desperation. "God, You've given me a pastor that is teaching me the Word and I appreciate that. But I also want a female mentor. One that will mentor me on how to become the leader You have called me to be."

Again and again she prayed similar prayers looking for God to bring that quality leader into her life. Finally she became frustrated with how long it was taking for God to answer her.

"God where is my mentor?"

God said, *I've already answered your request long ago. Your mentor is already in your life.*

Excitedly she asked, "Oh Lord, then who is it?"

He responded, *Its Diane Gardner.*

"What? Her? But she laughs too much to be my mentor. She can be silly. Besides we're the *same* age and she's a friend who sometimes her personality frustrates me. So how can she mentor me?"

The Holy Spirit answered, *Nevertheless Diane is your mentor and the one who will help you find the call of God for your life.*

She reluctantly shared her conversation with God about me. We decided we were opposite temperaments and personalities. And of course, I laughed. Then I shared a couple of important bits of wisdom with her God had given me for her but said I was not to share it until she wanted to hear.

Who is it that God may have ready to give you wisdom but prefer not to hear it from them?

Over thirty years later Betty is still my beautician and has risen to be a powerful leader in the Body of Christ. At major junctures in her life over these years God has impressed me with a word of wisdom for her. He has consistently used me in her life as that voice of wisdom, predominately to be a confirmation of God's timing in her life. Recently she checked back in with the Lord on the same subject.

"God what are you saying to me now about Diane in my life?"

God answered, *I'm still using Diane in your life.*

He spoke to me to share more vital things with her for pray and now she is one of my main intercessors.

The best part about her not missing God by her familiarity with His choice for a mentor is that God has used her profoundly in my life also over the years.

It was smart of her to check back in with God because we want to be current with who He wants to speak into our lives. We don't want to presume because God used someone for a season that the person should hold that position for infinity and beyond.

We also don't want to miss God because we have presumed who He cannot use because of our familiarity. Nazareth missed their visitation. They presumed and it led to familiarity which caused them not to accept who God had sent.

So often I see husbands tune out their wives words of wisdom because he hears her voice all the time. I see wives not understand a man's way of communicating and ignore or degrade his wisdom because it sounds like he is only complaining. If we want God to give us guidance we must submit to those who are around us.

Often I pray for the Holy Spirit to make me more aware of when He speaks to me. Sometimes I hear the same complaint from three people over a two week period. Why were they all saying the same thing? Because God was getting my attention that this was the next thing He wanted to prune from my life.

Sometimes I get defensive because I'm feeling the pressure of their dissatisfaction or they tell me what they don't like in a not-so-nice way. That's when my familiarity with them shuts down God's voice to me through them.

If we want truth from God we must give Him the privilege of using whoever He can.

People sometimes want to be friends with their pastor or spiritual leader but don't have an understanding of not crossing the line of over familiarity that reduces their leaders "right" to correct them. It's too bad human nature is like that. It takes a person truly submitted to God to allow Him to speak correction to us with someone we see as a peer.

We can ask the Holy Spirit to help us keep familiarity from causing us to miss Him.

Can God use someone you consider to be "crazy" or "ignorant" to speak into your life?

Eight Rs That Uncover Truth

Chapter Eleven

The wise will hear and increase their learning, And the person of understanding will acquire wise counsel and the skill [to steer his course wisely and lead others to the truth] (Proverbs 1:5 AMP).

Presumption can be a blanket we add on top of the truth. The real truth is not subject to our feelings, preferences, comfort zones, or fears. Truth is just that—truth. It is raw, revealing, refreshing, and restorative. Truth is also a person, Jesus Christ, the Messiah.

Jesus said to him, "I am the way, the truth, and the life. No one comes to the Father except through Me" (John 14:6).

When we are born again, Jesus, who is Truth Himself, resides on the inside of us. Our mission then is to learn to open up our hearts and minds to hear and respond to truth.

Our quest is to continually seek truth as He says it and not truth as we see it.

Presumption will always come but we can recognize it and conquer it. Let's decide to presumption-proof and deception-proof our walk in Christ. Here is the formula: Love God, love truth, and love God's Word more than you love being right in your own eyes and having your own way.

This is true surrender. When we feel God could not possibly have a different view of a person, situation, or our opinion, then we are presuming. It is good for us to decide that we choose to love God and surrender every opinion no matter how well formed and well informed we are. To be able to say to the Lord, "I really feel this is the right thing to do. Nevertheless, I surrender my conclusion to You because I love You even though I feel I'm right. You have the final word on this."

Our goal is to be aligned in truth—spirit, soul, and body. When all three are responding to truth we are at peace even when circumstances say the opposite. When we no longer look to our own opinion to evaluate what is truth, but instead look to the Bible and the Spirit of Christ within us, we will find ourselves right more times than wrong. That's good news!

Behold, You desire truth in the inward parts, and in the hidden part You will make me to know wisdom (Psalm 51:6 NKJ).

This passage talks about the hidden part of us and to know wisdom in the core of our being. Because we have chosen to act upon that truth, we will reap the benefits.

We are a triune being, and each part of us has a voice. Remember we are a spirit, we have a soul (mind, will, and emotions) and we live in a body.

If we want to increase our capacity to hear God's voice we must recognize when our other voices are speaking. Our mind has natural understanding and relies on our intellect. The voice of our emotions can be good or bad, based on whether they have been trained to respond to the nature of God or fear, anxiety, fear of death, etc. Our will has a voice and we can choose to submit to the Word or submit our will to stubbornness, rebellion, or our own preferences. Our body is a piece of meat with appetites so its voice always wants to feed one of its appetites. Your spirit always wants to agree with and obey God. God's voice never says anything different from the Word.

God desires truth from the inside out. He wants our spirit to operate from a place of truth and be in agreement with the Spirit of Truth within us. That's why we feed our spirit the truth of God's Word.

*However, when He, the **Spirit of truth**, has come, He will guide you into all **truth**; for He will not speak on His own authority, but whatever He hears He will speak; and He will tell you things to come* (John 16:3).

We can humble ourselves to the truth no matter how hard it is to hear or through whom it comes. If we do this then presumption will not have dominion over us and we will overcome presumption and deception.

Now no chastening seems to be joyful for the present, but painful; nevertheless, afterward it yields the peaceable fruit of righteousness to those who have been trained by it (Hebrews 12:11).

We can be trained to receive God's chastening which mainly comes through His Word. I remember year ago when the Lord told me I needed to learn to receive His chastening without fainting, defending, or condemning myself. If I submitted to that then

He would teach me some hard lessons that would give me great wisdom, insight and understanding.

We know we can trust God but I believe He is looking for those who want Him to be able to trust them. He wants to share with us more than we realize.

Here are the eight steps that remove the blanket of presumption and uncover my antidote of truth.

1. **Recognize** you are presuming. You've thought surely this is true, and you find out it's not. You catch yourself saying, "I thought," or "But I thought surely this was going to happen." This is the first step. You are on your way to freedom!
Stop right here! Say, "I've just presumed on that person, situation, or God. No one is obligated to what I have presumed. No matter how important it is to me."

2. **Repentance** is mandatory to recover from presumption. Obviously the truth is different from what you thought, even if what you thought was more integral, reasonable, or expeditious. It still is not what happened or what the other person wanted. Forgive yourself for presuming and forgive them. An example of a prayer is: Lord, forgive me for presuming on [God, yourself, or name the person].

No matter how you feel at this time your feelings will keep you angry or discouraged if you don't fully repent for presuming without justifying your presumption. Our natural soulish defense wants to say: I repent, but they are equally as wrong. Or I repent for presuming but they still should have done what I was thinking.

This is not true repentance. The subject here is not the right or wrong of the problem.

3. **Renounce** any bad fruit that can result from your presuming. An example is: I renounce whatever ammunition I have given the Enemy to use against me or others through this presumption. I renounce presumption and its right to have dominion over me and bring about detrimental circumstances.

According to Psalm 19:13, *Keep back Your servant also from presumptuous sins; Let them not have dominion over me. Then I shall be blameless, And I shall be innocent of great transgression.*

4. **Release** anyone from being accountable to you for your presumption: God, yourself, or others.
I will not hold God, myself, or _____ accountable to me for my presumption. There is no apology expected and no need for justification of anyone's actions.

5. **Responsibility** is all mine for the meditations in the back of my mind. I take full responsibility for any opinions and actions I have taken as a result of my presumption. If necessary I will repent to the person(s). We should say, "I presumed regarding you. Please forgive me." There will be no need to say what the presumption was, so I don't give place to the Enemy to use my words to cause more problems.

Example of what to say: I take responsibility for my presuming, and I need to make some changes.

6. **Resist** the adversary who is the believer's accuser. Revelation 12:10 names him the accuser who throws accusations at you about you, at you about others, at others about you, and at you about God.

Then I heard a loud voice saying in heaven, "Now salvation, and strength, and the kingdom of our God, and the power of His Christ have come, for the accuser of our brethren, who accused them before our God day and night, has been cast down (Revelation 12:10).

Satan can't hear our thoughts. His demons can see our actions and hear our words and they are familiar with us and our background.

Declaration: Satan, because of what is written in Revelation 12:10, I resist every accusation toward me and others because you are the accuser. I resist everywhere I have judged God's motives or the motives of others. In the Name of Jesus I cast down every high thought that exalts itself against the knowledge of God's Word.

I submit to God and resist the devil. James 4:7 says: *Therefore submit to God. Resist the devil and he will flee from you.*

7. **Rejoice** by finding things that are funny about your presumption. Rejoice you didn't make a complete fool of yourself, and if you did and you're totally embarrassed, the best way to kill that pride is to laugh in its face. Rejoice that you've read this book and do not continue to allow presumption to keep you frustrated. You're Free to recognize it and conquer it.

8. **Recover** truth as much as possible. Restoration does not mean things can go back to the way they were. But it does give you a fresh start, a healthy paradigm shift. Don't let shame, guilt, or condemnation make you think you cannot recover truth.

Be sensitive to God's timing. He will set the stage if you are willing to walk out on it.

Behold, I send you out as sheep in the midst of wolves. Therefore be wise as serpents and harmless as doves (Matthew 10:16).

Laugh at what previously upset you when you presumed. Say, here comes that old "I thought surely" again. Sometimes you and God can have a good laugh. He's not laughing at you, but with you. In Psalm 2:1-4 we see Satan's presumption and God's response, which is laughter. I love it!

*Why do the nations rage, And the people plot a vain thing? The kings of the earth set themselves, And the rulers take counsel together, Against the Lord and against His Anointed, saying, "Let us break Their bonds in pieces And cast away Their cords from us." He who sits in the heavens shall **laugh**; The Lord shall hold them in derision.*

A happy heart is good medicine and a joyful mind causes healing (Proverbs 17:22a).

Your mind has released thoughts you've held for years. You've expanded your capacity to receive from God and His Word. You now have more room to experience greater joy and a new freedom to sing a new song to the Lord and rejoice with Him as He rejoices over you.

Why not make up a song about His love for you and His goodness in bringing fresh truth into your life.

You have joined Him as He sings and rejoices over you.

The Lord your God in your midst,
The Mighty One, will save;
He will rejoice over you with gladness,
He will quiet you with His love,
He will rejoice over you with singing
(Zephaniah 3:17).

About the Author

Diane Gardner is a speaker, marketplace mentor, chaplain, and a grace expert. She is the author of *Overcoming the Enemy's Storms, featured book signings at Women of Faith,* contributing writer to *Forgive, Let Go, and Live, Breaking Invisible Chains: The Way to Freedom From Domestic Abuse*, and *Walking in Your Destiny Moving Through the Fear*. God's anointing through Diane is unique, powerful, and candid. Diane is founder of Overcomer's Conferences, Holy Spirit Encounter Marketplace Retreats, and Beautiful Women of God Seminars. She serves on international advisory boards of Christian Women in Media Association (CWIMA), Women United in Ministry (Mujeres Unidas en

Ministerio), and Liberty Savard Ministries. Diane is mother to two sons and grandmother to five; she resides in Riverside, California.

For speaking engagements, interviews, or to contact Diane, go to

<u>Godshouseoffavor@gmail.com</u> and
<u>www.beautifulwomenofGod.org</u>